Coins and Medals
of the
English Civil War

Edward Besly

Numismatist, National Museum of Wales

in association with
THE NATIONAL MUSEUM OF WALES

© National Museum of Wales
First published 1990

Typeset by Setrite Typesetters
Printed by Biddles Ltd., Guildford,
Surrey, Great Britain
for the publishers
B A Seaby Ltd
7 Davies Street
London W1Y 1LL

Distributed by
B T Batsford Ltd
P O Box 4, Braintree, Essex CM7 7QY

A CIP Catalogue record
for this book is available
from the British Library

ISBN 1 85264 065 0

Contents

List of Colour Plates
(between pp. 58–59)

Preface and Acknowledgements

A steady stream of articles and notes on the coinage of Charles I reflects both its numismatic interest and the regular appearance of new material from hoards and single finds in England and Wales; but apart from the highly-condensed specialist introduction to the Brooker collection (*Sylloge of Coins of the British Isles* 33, 1984) there is no general account of the coinages of the English Civil War and their context. I hope that this book will go some way to fill this gap, for general as well as specialist readers.

I should like to thank the following for permission to reproduce copyright photographs of objects and documents in their care: The Ashmolean Museum, Oxford (**47**); The City of Bristol Museum and Art Gallery (**56**); The British Library (**16, 25, 33, 34, 100, 110, 129**); The Trustees of the British Museum (**17, 49, 51, 106, 107, 108, 111, 115, 116, 119, 122, 124, 130, 131, 141, 145,** C.P. **II, IV** and **VI**); The Rector and Fellows of Exeter College, Oxford (**32, 41**); The Trustees of the National Gallery, London (C.P. **I**); The National Portrait Gallery, London (C.P. **X**); The Society of Antiquaries of London (**40**); Michael Doe (**77**); Sir Ralph Verney, Bt., for permission to photograph and reproduce the portrait of Ormonde (**121**); and especially Sir John Vyvyan, Bt. and Ferrers Vyvyan, Esq., for lending a transparency of Sir Richard Vyvyan, 1st Bt. (C.P. **VII**) and for permission to reproduce this and Vyvyan's 1643/4 mint commission (**72**), photography of which was kindly arranged by Caroline Humphreys of Cornwall Record Office.

All other coins and medals are in the National Museum of Wales, Cardiff and I am grateful to my colleagues Kevin Thomas for his excellent photographs, and Colin Williams, who drew the maps, 'feathers' and privy-marks. I am indebted to Sir Colin Cole, K.C.V.O., T.D., F.S.A., Garter King of Arms, for the information relating to the possible identity of Sir Thomas Cary. Also to George Boon, Barrie Cook, Joe Cribb, Tony Daly, Virginia Hewitt, John Kenyon and Fiona Runnalls, for their help at various stages; and not least to Peter Clayton and B.A. Seaby Ltd.

All coins and medals are reproduced at their natural size (monochrome) or twice lifesize (colour), except where indicated.

EDWARD BESLY
Department of Archaeology & Numismatics
National Museum of Wales

A Note on Dates and Prices

At the time of the Civil War, England and Wales used the Old Style (Julian) calendar, which ran ten days behind the New Style (Gregorian) dating – widely used on the Continent but not formally adopted in Britain until 1752, by which time the gap had increased to eleven days. The New Style year began on 1 January; but the English official year started on Lady Day, 25 March, so English documents and coins (where they bore dates) produced between 1 January and 24 March inclusive bear the 'previous' year's date, 1 January 1642 *following* 31 December 1642, for instance. The receipt for Exeter College's plate (**41**) is a good example.

Here, I have retained the Old Style days and months, as recorded by English contemporaries, but for dates between 1 January and 24 March inclusive, the years are expressed in a hybrid form, e.g. 1642/3, a method similar to that commonly used in the ensuing century.

The monetary system of England and Wales was until 1971 based on the Pound (£) of twenty shillings (s), each of twelve pence (d). Today we retain the pound as unit, but there all similarity to the money of the 1640s ends. Inflation, decimalization, and a very different economic way of life make comparisons difficult, but with all due caution we may suggest that the pound of the 1640s was the rough equivalent of £75 in 1989. This factor puts the cost of war in a new perspective, for which one example suffices here. Sir Richard Vyvyan calculated that he laid out £9,982 for the King's service, including the costs of compounding and of lawsuits – in today's terms, nearly £3/4 million. For individual prices, especially of everyday goods and services, the reader is referred to contemporary diaries and account-books, of which three Yorkshire examples are given under *Further Reading*.

Chapter 1

Prologue

Periods of conflict or uncertainty tend to yield numerous money hoards compared with times of peace and prosperity, and nowhere is this more true than of England and Wales during the Civil War, or 'Great Rebellion', in the reign of Charles I (1625–49). Thus during the Stuart period, an average of only about one hoard has been recorded for every year of the reigns of James I (1603–25), Charles II (1660–85) and even for the first dozen years of Charles I. But the decade 1639–49 has yielded 115 hoards which can be dated securely and at least another 80 likely to come from this period, but which are only recorded vaguely in old newspaper reports. For ordinary men and women, such wealth as they possessed consisted mainly of coins of the precious metals, silver and gold; there were no banks or building societies. So, when civil war broke out in 1642, many hid their cash in secure places, perhaps because they went off to fight, perhaps to avoid the exactions imposed by both sides. Occasionally we hear about the recovery of such assets: late in 1645, the royalist Sir Henry Slingsby managed to collect £40 in gold from his home near York, then deep in enemy territory. Others were less fortunate: death or enforced absence prevented many of them from recovering their goods.

Today chance, with or without electronic assistance, continues to bring these caches to light and few years pass without the discovery in England of one or more 'Civil War hoards', such as the one gold and 3,262 silver coins, with a total face value of £160 1s 0d, found in February 1987 at Ryhall, Rutland (now part of Leicestershire); or the 30 gold and 1,552 silver coins (£93 5s 0d) found at Breckenbrough, near Thirsk (North Yorkshire) in June 1985, which also provided evidence for local royalist provisioning in the form of receipts for cheese taken from two local farms in January 1643/4. There are many lesser deposits. Wales, smaller and infinitely poorer, has nevertheless produced at least a dozen hoards, including two substantial but ill-recorded finds from Conwy and Prestatyn in the north, a hoard of 105 coins found at Penybryn Hall, near Wrexham in 1979 (which included examples from five different royalist mints), and the more modest 35 silver coins found in the ruins of a farm building near Pontypridd, Mid-Glamorgan, in September 1988.

Coins are therefore some of the commonest relics of this crucial and much-studied phase of British history. The aim of this book is to explore the coinage produced by the two sides in the conflict and especially how the royalists, denied the Mint at the Tower of London, set about producing their own coin of the realm. This was not used in isolation, but locally supplemented the Tower coin in circulation, and we shall examine this first.

Coinage in early Stuart England and Wales

Almost all of the money circulating at the start of the Civil War had been produced at the Tower of London, which during the later Tudor and early Stuart periods housed the sole official mint; much of it had been produced many decades prior to 1642 (1–7). The history of English coinage is characterized by long periods of stability in denominations, weight and alloy standards, even design, with occasional adjustments in response to changing bullion prices or a new reign. To judge from the hoards, the earliest silver coins still in regular circulation were the good silver coins reintroduced in 1551 to put an end to a decade of severe debasements under Henry VIII and Edward VI (1, 2). Likewise, few gold coins dating from before Elizabeth I's reign were available for saving. The reason lies partly in the adoption of a new, and lower, fineness (22 carats, or 91.6%, as against 23 ct 3¼ grains, 99.5%) for gold coins in the later sixteenth century, the old standard being re-

Figs. 1–2 Edward VI, silver sixpence, privy-mark *Tun*, 1551–3; Philip and Mary, silver groat (4d), p.m. *Fleur-de-Lys*, 1554–7. Two of the earliest coins from the 1979 Penybryn (Wrexham) Treasure Trove, buried in 1644–5, showing the wear and other abuse resulting from ninety years or more of circulation.

tained for the Angel (10s) struck in minute quantities for the ceremony of 'touching for the King's Evil' (scrofula).

Large discoveries of silver in Central Europe (the Tyrol, the Erzgebirge and in Saxony) and Spain's New World colonies at the end of the fifteenth century led to massive increases in the available amounts of precious metal and one result was the production of the larger coins required for a rising level of international trade – and rising prices. Already by 1500 silver coins weighing up to one ounce were being

Fig. 3 Elizabeth I, silver shilling, p.m. *Scallop*, 1585−7; from the 1934 Prestatyn Treasure Trove, buried in 1643.

Fig. 4 Elizabeth I, silver sixpence, p.m. *Tun*, dated 1593. The rose behind the Queen's head and the added date served to distinguish the sixpence and its fractions (3d, 1½d, ¾d) from similar-sized coins of the groat series (4d, 2d, 1d) which were not so marked. (Prestatyn Treasure Trove).

struck by the producer states in Austria and Germany as substitutes for gold coins of the same value. The new large types caught on more slowly in other areas, especially on the fringes of Europe. In England the groat (fourpenny piece) had long been the largest silver coin. In 1504 Henry VII had made an experimental issue of testoons or shillings of twelve pence, but testoons did not become a regular part of the currency until the debasements of the 1540s. In 1560−1, when Elizabeth I caused the base monies of Henry VIII and Edward VI to be recoined, shillings were produced in large quantities as a matter of minting convenience. During much of the rest of her reign, the sixpence was the leading silver coin and these two denominations, with their equivalents produced under James I, often make up a large part of the value of hoards deposited during the Civil War (**3−5; Colour Plate II**).

Bigger coins still, halfcrowns (2s 6d) and crowns of five shillings were first produced in 1551−3. Others were coined late in Elizabeth's reign and for James I, but quantities were small. Only during the 1630s did the silver halfcrown (**9**) become an important coin in regular circulation, as a result of an arrangement whereby a proportion of the

Fig. 5 James I, silver shilling of 2nd coinage, p.m. *Fleur-de-Lys*, 1604–5. The reverse legend 'Whom God hath joined, let no man put asunder' refers to the personal union of England and Scotland. James adopted the title 'King of Great Britain' in October 1604. (Prestatyn Treasure Trove).

silver needed to pay Spain's troops in the Netherlands was from 1632 transported in English ships, via Dover, taking advantage of England's neutrality in the European ('Thirty Years') war. (This agreement was quite separate from the 'Cottington' treaty of 1630 and was probably the work of Arthur Hopton, the Secretary at Madrid.) At Dover, two-thirds were unloaded and sent to the Mint at London, where Spanish agents paid the necessary charges and then used the recoined silver to buy bills of exchange redeemable in Flanders. The remaining third (increased to two-thirds in 1638) was re-exported directly, against a duty of 1½ per cent. The result was a dramatic increase both in the Mint's output of silver (a mere £143,000 in the six years 1626–32 became nearly £4 million, or about 475 tons of silver coins, in the decade 1632–42) and in the amount of silver circulating in England and Wales, coupled with a massive drain of gold to the Continent as debts were settled there using the higher value metal, which was much

Fig. 6 James I, gold Unite of 22 shillings, 2nd coinage, p.m. *Book*, 1616–17. The name 'Unite' was ordained by proclamation, 16 November 1604. The rising price of gold relative to silver forced the Unite to be raised from 20s to 22s in 1612 and by 1661 it was valued at 23s 6d.

less bulky to transport. As a correspondent noted in 1652, 'we have in Amsterdam more English gold than you have yourselves in all England, this gold hath been all sent within twenty years ...' and this is echoed both in the Civil War hoards, the vast majority of which consist solely of silver coins, or at most contain one or two of gold, and the frequency with which weights for English gold appear in the sets used by Flemish and Dutch merchants to check those passing most commonly through their hands (6–8).

Fig. 7 James I, gold 20 shillings, or 'Laurel', 3rd coinage, p.m. *Rose*, 1620–1. New, lighter, gold coins proclaimed on 31 July 1619 remedied the 'perplexities in reckoning' occasioned by the 1612 revaluation and restored gold coins of 5s, 10s and 20s 'stamped on the one side with Our picture crowned with a Laurell'.

Fig. 8 Charles I, gold crown (five shillings), p.m. *Feathers*, 1630–1. Charles's gold continued the standards of James I's third ('laurel') coinage.

Fig. 9 Charles I, silver halfcrown, p.m. *Crown*, 1635–36/7, from the Penybryn hoard. The reverse legend ('I reign by Christ's favour') alludes to Charles's belief in the divine right of Kings, and appears on the four largest silver types (5s, 2s 6d, 1s, 6d.).

Of the coins for everyday use at the lower end of the scale, only groats are found in any quantity in hoards, though silver pieces down to the unmanageably small halfpenny are sometimes encountered (pence (**10**) and halfgroats are frequently found on their own, representing casual losses). Official coinage in copper had yet to be developed, but the City of Bristol had issued square copper farthing tokens under licence from the Crown during Elizabeth's reign. Royal copper-alloy farthing tokens, first authorized in 1613, were made under licence by a sequence of noble contractors, ostensibly to ease small transactions and to aid poor relief, in practice for their own profit (**11**). These, too, are found today in large numbers; they were frequently counterfeited and were alleged to have been produced by the royalists in Bristol during the Civil War.

Fig. 10 Charles I, silver penny, p.m. *Fleur-de-Lys*, 1625–6. Later Tower Mint pence bore the King's portrait and the royal arms.
Fig. 11 Copper farthing in the name of Charles I. 'Rose' type, produced under licence from 1636 by Lord Maltravers and Sir Francis Crane.

In their designs, the Tudor coinages retained some vestiges of the uniform medieval types, notably in using a cross as the basic element of the reverse. However, portraits had become naturalistic (**3**) and other modernizing features, such as Roman lettering, coats of arms, statements of value and even the date (**4**), had all appeared by 1600. From Elizabeth I onwards, we may also note the left and right alternation of the royal portraits from reign to reign, which to the present day remains a feature of British coinage (e.g. **3, 5, 8**). Although the basic designs and legends were prescribed, they could be treated in many different ways, depending on the engraver. We shall see this, for instance, in the equestrian effigies on the crowns and halfcrowns, of which we shall encounter many, few of which could be described as realistic when compared with a painted likeness (**Colour Plate I**), although the constraints of working within a circular frame, and of giving suitable prominence to the figure of the King, should be acknowledged.

The circulating medium was completed by small quantities of coins from other countries, such as the Scots gold (**12**) and silver (**13**) brought by James VI and I and his retinue to London following his English accession, declared legal tender in England by proclamation on

Fig. 12 James VI, gold sword-and-sceptre piece (£6 Scots), 8th Coinage, Edinburgh 1602. Proclaimed legal tender in England and Wales at ten shillings in 1603.

Fig. 13 James VI, silver thistle merk (13s 4d Scots), Eighth coinage, Edinburgh 1602. Legal tender in England and Wales at 13½d in 1603, together with its half- and quarter-pieces (6¾d and 3½d?).

8 April 1603; and the shillings and sixpences struck at the Tower Mint between 1603 and 1607 for use in Ireland (**14**). The silver types, unfamiliar in design and awkwardly valued, seem to have been coins people were happy to be rid of − part of the Ship Money tax collected in Monmouthshire in 1639 was described by the Sheriff as 'such ragged pieces as broken groats, quarter pieces of thirteenpence half-pennies, . . . , harpers, and fourpence halfpennies . . . the which I intend,

Fig. 14 James I, shilling for Ireland, London, p.m. *Martlet*, 1604−5. Legal tender in England and Wales at ninepence, being of sterling silver but only three-quarters of the weight of its English counterpart. The Irish sixpence was also current, at 4½d.

God willing, to change into good money or gold'. Post-Union Scots coins, of both James VI and Charles I, were the exact equivalents of their English counterparts in weights, standards and general design, and mingled happily into English circulation at an exchange rate of 12 shillings Scots to one shilling English (e.g., **21**).

From time to time it was deemed expedient to allow certain Continental types to circulate in England and Wales, notably following royal marriages. In 1554 Mary Tudor made a range of Spanish gold and silver coins legal tender at valuation, and although Elizabeth I promptly banned it, Spanish silver seems to have been tolerated in England into the seventeenth century. In 1613 James I forbade the use of clipped Spanish silver, which disrupted the 'benefit previously brought to trade' by the use of Spanish coins of full weight. Nevertheless, heavily-worn silver reals and half-reals of the sixteenth century appear from time to time in hoards of the Civil War years.

The dowry brought by Henrietta Maria on her marriage to Charles in 1625 included 'good summes of money of the coyne of France', whose recoinage was frustrated by an outbreak of the plague in London. Accordingly, the silver 'cardecue' (quart d'écu) was proclaimed legal tender at nineteenpence halfpenny on 4 September 1625 (**15**). Importing of light cardecues was strictly forbidden, but proved impossible to control. On 6 July 1626, for instance, the Mayor of Newcastle reported to the Privy Council that in May searchers had confiscated 2,178 cardecues which French merchants had used to buy coal. They were generally found to be light, and not worth above 16d. Shortly afterwards, on 24 July, the cardecue was demonetized, though its use lingered on a little while. On 2 January 1626/7, one Stephen Morrell of Colne deposed that he had been robbed at Preston fair on 28 October 1626 of a purse containing 46 shillings, three 'cartdekues' and a broken shilling.

Fig. 15 France, Henri IV (1589–1610), silver quart d'écu or 'cardecue', Bayonne mint (identified by letter L below the reverse shield), 1598. Legal tender in England and Wales at 19½d, 1625–6. (See also **100**).

Coin manufacture

The production of coinage was strictly controlled by contract between the Crown and the Master-Worker(s) of the Mint. Bullion brought to the Mint was purchased at a set price, turned into coinage whose denominations were specified and whose weights and alloy standards were fixed within narrow limits (see Table I), and reissued subject to defined charges to cover minting costs and profits and the King's 'royalty' or seigniorage. By way of safeguard, samples were withdrawn at random from every 'journey' of coins (30 lb in the case of silver) and sealed in a box for regular, roughly annual, 'trials of the pyx' at which weight and fineness were tried by a jury drawn from the London Goldsmiths' Company. To this end all of the dies were given a 'privy-mark', a private symbol sometimes described today as a mint- or initial-mark, which also serves to date the coins, since before 1649 only a minority of English coins incorporated an explicit date in their designs. This mark − a harp, a crown, a scallop-shell (the coins illustrated and Table II, of Charles I's Marks, give an idea of the variety of choices) − was appended at the master-worker's orders in accordance with his indenture with the Crown: 'he . . . shall be holden and bound to make a privy mark to all the moneys that shall be made by him so that if need should be he may know and discern which moneys . . . amongst others be made by him and which not . . .' as Thomas Bushell's 1637 indenture for the Aberystwyth Mint puts it.

Table I: *The English Monetary System of Charles I, 1625−42*

GOLD (Tower Mint only)	SILVER
22 ct fine (91.6%)	*11 oz 2 dwt fine* (92.5%)
Twenty shillings, 41 to the Troy pound	Five shillings, or Crown (Tower only)
Ten shillings	Two shillings and sixpence, or Halfcrown
Five shillings	Shilling, 62 to the Troy pound
23 ct 3¼ gr fine (99.5%)	Sixpence
Ten shillings (Angel), 89 to the Troy pound (for ceremonial use)	Fourpence, or Groat (Aberystwyth only)
	Threepence (Aberystwyth only)
	Twopence
	Penny
	Halfpenny

N.B.   One pound (£) = twenty shillings, each of twelve pence (d)
One Troy pound weight = twelve ounces
One Troy ounce = 20 pennyweights = 480 grains
= 31.10 grammes; 1 gramme = 15.43 grains

Table II: *Tower Mint privy-marks and pyx trials of Charles I, from 1625 until 1643*

♣	Lys	29 June 1626
♟	Cross on steps	27 April 1627
	Negro head	27 April 1627
	Castle	3 July 1628
⚓⚓	1st Anchor	26 June 1629
♡	Heart	23 June 1630
	Feathers	30 June 1631
	Rose	21 June 1632
	Harp	11 July 1633
	Portcullis	27 June 1634
	Bell	18 June 1635
	Crown	14 Feb 1636/7
	Tun	8 May 1638
⚓	2nd Anchor	4 July 1639
△	Triangle	26 July 1640
✸	Star	15 July 1641
◉	Triangle-in-circle	29 May 1643
	Briot's coinages	
B ❀	Flower, with B	1631–2
⚓	Anchor, with B or a mullet	1638–9

The control of fineness and weight was of great importance for both gold and silver, since the face values of the coins were closely related to the intrinsic value of their metal, unlike our own today, which are mere tokens. For silver the fineness, which was measured in terms of the Troy (12 ounce) pound weight of finished metal, was set at 11 ounces and 2 pennyweights, with 18 dwt of 'alloy' — in modern terms 92.5% of pure metal, or sterling silver; gold coins for circulation were 22 carats (91.6%) fine. Because precision was hard to achieve, a variation (the 'remedy') was allowed both in weight and fineness, of two pennyweight in the pound (0.833%) either side of the standard.

Tudor and early Stuart coinage stands at the end of a long tradition of production by manual methods. The sequence of operations, some of which are shown in **16**, was long and complicated: bullion was first melted, assayed and adjusted to the correct fineness and then cast into thin ingots, which were reduced to the required thickness by a sequence of beatings and annealings; blanks were cut and further annealed, then stacked and hammered to an approximately circular shape. After more annealing they were blanched by boiling in an acid solution ('argol' – potassium tartrate from the lees of wine) and turned into coin by hammering between two engraved dies. The dies themselves were made of iron with steeled faces (**17**). Designs were 'engraved' on their

Fig. 16 Minting at the Tower of London, depicted by Holinshed (1577). The activities shown here – weighing of bullion and the cutting, annealing (or blanching), hammering and coining of the blanks – were in practice carried out in separate workshops. On the extreme right coins are produced by hammering blanks between two iron dies. *British Library.*

faces using small positive punches, a technique used since Anglo-Saxon times; by now larger elements such as the King's head were formed from single punches, so giving the coinage a certain uniformity

(Shown at twice lifesize)

Fig. 17 Two views of an iron coining die for gold ten-shillings of Charles I, p.m. *Heart*, 1629–30. This is a lower, or pile die, whose spike helped to anchor it in a block or bench. It was recovered from the Thames foreshore in 1983. The face has not been hardened and the die may never have been used. *British Museum.*

of appearance. The lower die, or pile, bore a spike by which it was anchored in a bench or block and was the die which bore the King's portrait; the upper die, or trussel, was hand held and received direct hammer blows. It therefore wore out faster than the other, two trussels on average being needed for every pile die that was made.

The sixteenth and seventeenth centuries saw a gradual transition in Europe to the use of machinery for some of these operations: rolling mills for the ingots, punches to cut out the blanks and devices for marking their edges, and the coining operation itself. These changes were prompted by aesthetic considerations, desire for improved efficiency, the technical problems of handling the increased amounts of precious metal reaching the mints, and the need to combat the twin menaces of clipping and counterfeiting.

The appearance of the finished coin was above all determined by the skill of the moneyers. The new large silver denominations of the sixteenth century were hard to strike satisfactorily by traditional methods, even though devices such as drop-hammers may have been used to increase the available power. Machines devised for the coining process used one of two methods, percussive striking or something akin to rotary printing. The former, which ultimately became universal, employed dies mounted in a screw press. The latter was essentially a modification of the rolling mill, whereby groups of dies were engraved on steel rollers, and the coins were produced by passing strips of metal between them. Some of the larger European mints, e.g. Segovia in Spain and Hall in the Tyrol, harnessed water power to drive both rolling mills and coining machines, though they could − up to a point − be worked by hand, since the designs were imprinted progressively as the strip passed through and less instantaneous force was required. Finished coins were punched out in a separate operation and, at Hall, tumbled in sand to remove rough edges. A variant of the rotary technique, probably developed in response to practical problems encountered with the 'roller' method, involved the use of a simple hand-operated machine. Here, single pairs of dies with curved surfaces were mounted in pockets on two parallel axles. Prepared blanks were fed between them to produce the coins. This type of machine is usually called a rocker press, which refers to the to-and-fro motion of the dies.

These mechanical innovations had largely passed England by (18). The only serious experiments with coining machines at the Tower Mint were made by two Frenchmen: from 1561 to 1572, Eloi Mestrelle

Fig. 18 Charles I, Tower shilling, p.m. *Heart*, 1629−30, with 'feathers' on the reverse referring to the use of Welsh silver. A characteristic hammer-struck coin showing slight doubling of parts of the legend as a result of repeated blows.

produced small quantities of 'milled' coin for Elizabeth I, probably using a simple screw-press (**19**). Rotary methods were known in London by the end of the century, but found use only in experiments for small change and in medal-making. In 1613, however, the newly-licensed royal farthing tokens were made 'exactly and artificially of copper, by Engins and instruments' using cylindrical 'roller' dies.

Fig. 19 Elizabeth I, shilling, p.m. *Star*, 1561–2, milled issue. Mestrelle's precise technique is not known, but he seems to have used a form of screw press.

In 1625 Nicholas Briot, engraver-general of the Paris Mint, came to London having fallen out with his masters. He was welcomed by Charles I and thereafter engraved most of the effigies for the Tower coinage. He also produced experimental issues of coins using rotary methods, in 1631–2 and 1638–9, but was dogged by teething troubles, notably in controlling the weights of individual coins. Like Mestrelle before him he failed to persuade the mint authorities to adopt his methods, despite the superior appearance of his products (**20**). Briot's work was also slow, and the need to coin large amounts of silver rapidly in the years after 1632 may explain their reluctance to pursue

Fig. 20 Charles I, silver crown by Nicholas Briot, p.m. *Flower*, 1631–2. A beautiful example of Briot's abilities as engraver and engineer, produced using a rotary (rocker) press.

Fig. 21 Charles I, 30-shillings Scots, Edinburgh 1637–42. Sir John Falconer's issue using a Briot rocker press. Perfection was less easily obtained in a routine production run, as can be seen by comparison with **20**. This was the exact equivalent of the English halfcrown of 30 pence.

this form of manufacture. However, in 1635 Briot was appointed Master of the Scottish mint and from 1637 was allowed to install and use his machinery at Edinburgh (**21**). When civil war threatened in 1642, Briot, by now back in London, and his assistant David Ramage prepared equipment for two proposed royalist mints, at Shrewsbury and York. The latter, as will be seen, used rotary methods, as did several other royalist mints in the Welsh Marches. Following further experiments under the Commonwealth and Protectorate, mechanized production was finally adopted at the Tower Mint in 1663. This survey of England's Civil War coinage thus neatly encompasses the halting progress of the country's coinage manufacture into the machine age.

Welsh silver and the Aberystwyth Mint

From a hesitant start under Elizabeth, but more consistently from 1623, late in James I's reign, small quantities of silver from the Mines Royal in Cardiganshire, refined from argentiferous lead on the spot, were shipped regularly to London to be coined at the Tower Mint. To publicize the Welsh mines, the coins were marked on the reverse, above the royal arms, with the feathers badge of the Prince of Wales (**22**), though in practice the highly-refined Welsh metal was melted together with other consignments to bring them up to the mint standard. Coins bearing the feathers were produced until 1638 (**23, 24**), and from 1627 until 1631 Wales was the source of almost all of the small amounts of silver coined in London, about £23,000 (**18**).

In 1636 the lease of the Cardiganshire Mines Royal was bought by Thomas Bushell (**25**), who proceeded to improve them using up-to-date drainage and mining techniques. Bushell petitioned to have a mint set up on the spot, in Aberystwyth Castle, and on 30 July 1637 he was empowered to proceed by letters patent in the form of an indenture

Figs. 22–24 Silver coins with the Welsh feathers: James
I, halfcrown, p.m. *Thistle*, 1621–3; Charles I, shilling,
p.m. *Bell*, 1634–5 and crown, p.m. *Tun*, 1636/7–38 (the
last mark to include Welsh silver struck in London under
Charles I). **22** comes from the Bridgewater House collection and **24** from that of Dr John Sharp, Archbishop of
York, both formed in the later part of the seventeenth
century.

between the King and himself. Repairs to the castle and the setting-up
of the mint were followed by the first delivery of silver ingots to the
moneyers on 18 January 1638/9. Procedures were similar to those of
the Tower Mint, except that all of the dies were engraved in London
and supplied ready for use. The mint had its own officers and a team
of three moneyers on secondment from the Tower, Bushell himself
combining the posts of Warden and Master-worker. Other labour was
recruited locally.

Fig. 25 Thomas Bushell, future Aberystwyth mint master, aged about 30. A woodcut from his *Youth's Errors*, 1628. *British Library*.

Figs. 26–27 Aberystwyth, shilling and groat, p.m. *Open Book*, 1639–42.

Bushell's indenture provided for the production of five of the same silver denominations as the Tower Mint: halfcrowns (**31**), shillings (**26**), sixpences, halfgroats (**28**) and pence (**29**), but not crowns or halfpence. A supplementary commission dated 22 February 1637/8 added the halfpenny (**30**), as well as groats (**27**) and threepences – a notable departure, perhaps intended to remedy the poor state of those already in circulation (**2**), since no groats had been coined since 1561 and no threepences since 1582. Certainly, these two denominations are the commonest Aberystwyth products surviving today. By Bushell's

Figs. 28–30 Aberystwyth, smaller coins: halfgroat, penny, halfpenny, with Welsh feathers prominent as reverse design (Tower Mint halfpence bore a rose on both sides).

Fig. 31 Aberystwyth, halfcrown, *c.* 1642. Its obverse die was among those taken to Shrewsbury by Bushell late in September of that year.

express wish, the feathers appeared on *both* sides (except on the twopence, penny and halfpenny (28–30), where they were the main feature of the reverse) and he chose an *open book* as his privy-mark, perhaps to denote that this new departure in providing coin had nothing to conceal, unlike so many Stuart monopolies. In a little over three and a half years, the mint produced around £10,500 in silver coin.

Chapter 2

Civil War

In the summer of 1642, England went to war with herself. The origins of this war and the political manoeuvrings of the 1640s have been much discussed elsewhere and are best described by the historian (see *Further Reading*). The purpose of this chapter is twofold: to give a very brief summary of the main events of the war; and to survey royalist minting in its geographical and operational context, as an introduction to the chapters that follow.

The progress of the War, 1642−6 (*see* Map 1)

Charles I left London on 10 January 1641/2 and in March established his court at York. In May he sent for the Great Seal, which was conveyed secretly to the King by its Keeper, Lord Lyttleton. War looked certain, though Charles was frustrated in his bid for arms stored at Hull, and broke out formally on 22 August, when the King raised his standard at Nottingham, and proceeded to Shrewsbury to recruit in Wales and the Marches. Both sides tried to secure the local militia and their arms. It was generally expected that a single campaign would settle matters, but the first major battle, at Edgehill on 23 October, was inconclusive. The royalists, advancing on London, sacked Brentford on 12 November but were then turned back by the capital's trained bands drawn up at Turnham Green. Charles established his wartime capital at Oxford.

1643 saw important royalist successes, notably the conquest of most of the West Country and the capture of Bristol. The Marquess of Newcastle, having finally overrun all of Yorkshire (except Hull) advanced into Lincolnshire, but his reluctance to move further afield cost the King his only opportunity to make inroads into East Anglia, where an anti-parliamentarian rising at Kings Lynn (July-August 1643) finally withered for lack of royalist support. Inability to combine their various armies in a concerted campaign frustrated the royalist advance on London, which was halted by the drawn first battle of Newbury (20 September). Meanwhile, parliamentarian strongholds such as Plymouth, Lyme Regis and especially Gloucester tied down forces and always threatened the royalist rear; the siege of Gloucester was relieved by the Earl of Essex on 5 September.

In attempting to force a solution, both sides sought help from outside, the King from Ireland, where an English army was countering the rebellion which had broken out in 1641, and Parliament, at great expense, from the Scots. An Anglo-Irish force of about 3,000 men arrived in north-east Wales late in November 1643, relieving pressure on the royalist garrison at Chester and taking part in several successful skirmishes, before being routed by Sir Thomas Fairfax and Sir William Brereton at Nantwich on 25 January 1643/4. The arrival of the Scots, however, was to prove one of the decisive factors which swung the war towards Parliament.

In 1644, although their western army was halted at Alresford in Hampshire on 29 March, the King's forces held their own in the south. One parliamentarian force was worsted at Cropredy, north of Oxford (6 June) and the invasion of the West by the Earl of Essex ended in disaster when the King trapped his army in Cornwall, though the investment of Taunton once again forced the royalists to waste men, materials and time in an unsuccessful siege. A second battle at Newbury (27 October) was again inconclusive.

In the north, however, a major royalist defeat at Selby (11 April) was followed by the arrival of the Scots and the siege of York. Prince Rupert, the King's nephew, after relieving Newark and conducting a lightning campaign in Lancashire, outwitted the besieging armies and relieved York on 1 July, but on the following day his army was shattered at Marston Moor, the largest set-piece engagement of the war, and the royalists lost the entire north of England. The winter saw a thorough overhaul of parliamentarian forces, with the creation of the New Model Army and its consequences. Sir Thomas Fairfax became Commander-in-Chief, with Oliver Cromwell as commander of the horse. Peace negotiations at Uxbridge came to nothing.

Despite the loss of Shrewsbury on 22 February 1644/5, the 1645 campaign seemed to start well for the royalists; but on 30−31 May Prince Rupert stormed and sacked Leicester, provoking a parliamentarian response which led directly to the battle of Naseby on 14 June. Here the King's field army was destroyed and his baggage and secret correspondence captured. The battle of Langport (10 July) and the fall of Bristol on 11 September opened the way to the West Country. The King continued to hope for help from outside, but mishandled negotiations with the Irish Catholics proved a great embarrassment, while the Marquess of Montrose's brilliant campaign in Scotland came to an end when he was beaten at Philiphaugh (south of Edinburgh) on 13 September. Mopping-up operations in England lasted well into 1646, Pendennis in Cornwall being the last royalist garrison to surrender, on 17 August. (In Wales, Harlech held out until 13 March 1646/7.) The King himself had slipped out of his besieged capital and surrendered to the Scots army near Newark on 5 May 1646.

Royalist minting: a survey (*see* Maps 2−4)

At first, most of the money required to clothe, feed, equip and above all to pay the King's army was raised in cash from his supporters as gifts or as loans at the standard rate of eight per cent *per annum*, or was seized from opponents. The King may have had an advantage over his adversaries here, since many of the wealthiest men supported him, notably the Marquess of Worcester at Raglan Castle and his heir Edward, Lord Herbert. There are also records of generous cash contributions from many individuals and from the universities of Oxford and Cambridge (32) − the frequently-repeated comment that the universities sent plate at this juncture may be somewhat misleading, since it is evident that some at least of the Oxford colleges borrowed large sums of money to make up their quota and only yielded their plate the following January. With a single short campaign in prospect, rates of pay could be generous and will have tempted those whose normal wages were only a few pence a day. The royalist Earl of Northampton offered as much as two shillings (24d) per day to raise a private army to besiege Warwick Castle, whose parliamentarian owner, Lord Brooke, paid his garrison 4s 8d per man per week (i.e. 8d per day). The latter sum was also offered by royalist recruiters at Myddle, in Shropshire, and seems to have become the standard rate for infantry, on both sides. Early in September (33), Sir John Byron offered a

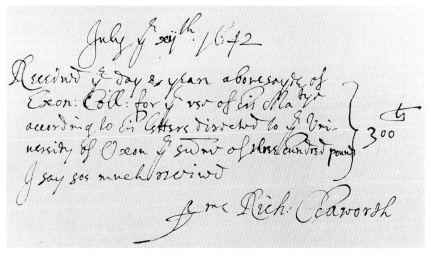

Fig. 32 Royalist fund-raising, 12 July 1642: a receipt signed by Dr Richard Chaworth, MP for Midhurst and Chancellor of the diocese of London, for £300 contributed by Exeter College in response to the King's appeal to Oxford University − £138 of which had to be borrowed (see p. 35). By 20 July, £10,000 from the University had reached the King at York. *Exeter College, Oxford.*

Proclamation.

 Hoſoever will ſerve the K I N G *as a foot Souldier, and bring his Muſ-ket, ſhall have pay* 6ˢ. per weeke. *Whoſoever will ſerve upon any* Nagge *or Mare of* 3ˡ. *price or up-ward as a* Dragoon, *and will bring a* Musket, *ſhall have pay* 12ˢ.10ᵈ. per weeke.

If he bring a Gun *of any other kind that is foure foot long hee ſhall have* 11ˢ.8ᵈ. per weeke.

Without a Gun 10ˢ.6ᵈ. per weeke.

Whoſoever will bring a ſerviceable Horſe, ſaddled and bridled, with Piſtoll *or* Carabin *ſhall have* 3ˡ. *towards his Horſe, and his Horſe his owne at the end of the ſer-vice, and* 17ˢ. 6ᵈ. per weeke.

Let them repaire to Sir I O H N B Y R O N *Colonell of a Regiment of Horſe for His* Majeſtie, *and all this ſhall be performed.*

God ſave the K I N G.

Fig. 33 A royalist recruiting poster, displayed at Oxford. Sir John (later Lord) Byron was colonel of the first horse regiment raised for the King and occupied the city from 28 August until 10 September 1642, gathering men and equipment. The high rate of pay for foot and the appeal for equipment suggest a date very early in the war, and the annotation indicates that the poster was displayed on Saturday, 3 September 1642. *British Library.*

better rate for foot (6s per week), but his basic pay of 1s 6d per day for dragoons and 2s 6d for cavalry (who had to provide for their horses) matches exactly the rates for these categories in the parliamentarian Eastern Association in 1644−5.

Much of the country's portable wealth was in the form of silver plate: this too was donated or 'lent'; a Receiver of Plate, Dr Stephen Goffe, was appointed at York on 3 August 1642, empowered to collect and give receipts for money or plate given or tendered for the King's service. Other sources of bullion included foreign coin (notably from the Low Countries, where the Queen worked tirelessly to raise loans), personal jewellery, prize-goods, and newly-mined Welsh silver, the last of which provided the royalists with a steady income of around £100 per week. Displaced from London, the royalists needed mints to convert these contributions into negotiable coin.

Active steps were taken by the royalists to establish mints in the provinces from the moment the King and his Court settled in York. The engraver Nicholas Briot was summoned to York and equipment was meanwhile prepared at the Tower Mint for use at the proposed mints of Shrewsbury and York. These were to be campaign mints designed to help establish and equip the King's field army. In the event, York could as yet play no useful part, but Shrewsbury's contribution was valuable in both practical and propaganda terms. A third mint, at Truro, owed its existence to the isolation of royalist Cornwall in the early months of the war. It too had its moment of usefulness as a campaign mint in the Spring of 1643. York, meanwhile, finally started production late in January 1642/3.

Although little documentary evidence survives concerning their operation, enough remains to demonstrate the important point that the royalist mints were established with full formality. York mint was set up by royal warrant at the time when the Court was based there; and the Earl of Newcastle's commission as Commander-in-Chief north of the Trent, issued in October 1642, included the power to coin money (**76**). Shrewsbury, and its successors at Oxford and then Bristol, operated as extensions of the Aberystwyth royal mint and no further authority was required. Thomas Bushell (**25**) and Sir William Parkhurst (**52**), erstwhile Warden of the Tower Mint, were named joint wardens of this group of mints. In Cornwall, Sir Richard Vyvyan (**Colour Plate VII**) received a commission to coin bullion or plate in November 1642. The three areas of royalist power were thus formally equipped with the authority required for coining.

When Edgehill proved inconclusive, both sides had to make more permanent financial arrangements as the scale of the war grew. The money needed to finance each season's campaigns was raised in various ways: by local assessments in the counties; from traditional revenues such as the Court of Wards (where these could be enforced); from the Customs of ports such as Bristol; from the Excise, invented by the Parliament in 1643 and imitated thereafter by the royalists; and from the appropriation of the assets of 'delinquents', as each side described the other's supporters. There were other fund-raising attempts, notably in February 1643/4 when the King sent 'privy seal' letters to known supporters, in an attempt to raise £100,000 for that year's campaign.

Developments in 1643 saw two major changes: a further branch mint of Aberystwyth was set up at Bristol from Oxford; and the Truro mint was transferred to Exeter, hard on the heels of the royalist capture of either city. A new commission regularizing the Exeter branch was subsequently issued to Vyvyan (**72**). Next, on 22 May 1644, Sir Thomas Cary received a commission to erect one or more mints in the counties of Hereford, Worcester, Shropshire and Chester; and it is likely, though unproved, that at least one mint operated in each (Hereford and Chester are attested by documents, Salop (Shrewsbury) only by coins). This extension of royalist minting arrangements may have arisen from the administrative reforms carried out by Prince Rupert following his appointment as Captain-General in the Welsh Marches in January 1643/4, which included an overhaul of the operation of local taxation. A further commission dated 29 July 1644 was issued to Edward, Lord Herbert, son of the Marquess of Worcester, to erect one or more mints (in South Wales?) but was not acted upon. In 1660, in a letter to the Earl of Clarendon, Herbert (better known as the Earl of Glamorgan) explained that his commitment in Ireland (where he had been secretly empowered by the King to negotiate with the Irish Catholics) had prevented him from using his minting powers.

We do not know the wording of Newcastle's commission which set York into motion, but the terms of the others are generally similar. Vyvyan was required to use 'dies, stamps and forms as the moneys now current within Our Realm of England' (November 1642) and more explicitly in his second commission (3 January 1643/4) 'to make and engrave ... Irons and Stampes with Our Effigies Inscriptions and Armes according to our present money in Our Tower of London'. Cary was authorized to coin 'moneys in such manner as in the Tower of London'. In the event, both Vyvyan and Cary followed the extended provisions of Bushell's Aberystwyth indentures in producing groats and threepences in addition to normal Tower denominations. (Threepences were also produced at York). Only occasionally, and perhaps for special reasons, did they produce the *Exurgat* designs (pp. 29, 31) character-istic of the 'Royal' series at Shrewsbury, Oxford and Bristol. For their pains, the royalist mintmasters were granted the same allowances as

Table III: *The Pattern of Royalist Minting, 1642–6*

	GOLD			SILVER									
	£3	20s	10s	20s	10s	5s	2s6d	1s	6d	4d	3d	2d	1d
Bushell/Parkhurst													
Shrewsbury 1642	?	+		+	+	+	+	+					?
Oxford 1642–3	+	+	+	+	+	+	+	+	+		?	?	
1644–6	+	+	+	+		+	+	+	+	+	+	+	+
Bristol 1643–5			+				+	+	+	+	+	+	+
A/B/Plumes 1645–6							+	+	+	+	+	+	+
Vyvyan													
Truro 1642–3		+ }			(+)	+	+	+					
Exeter 1643–5		+ }				+	+	+	+	+	+	+	+
Newcastle													
York 1643–4							+	+	+		+		
Cary													
W/SA series 1644–6		+					+	+	+	+	+	+	
Chester 1644–5?		+					+	+			+		
HC							+						
CH							+						
'Declaration'							+						
'Garter'													

were paid at the Tower, and without having to present their accounts. The local commander's note of receipt discharged the master's responsibilities.

Mint practice differed from that at the Tower in that there was no provision for a trial of the pyx, though Bushell's Aberystwyth indenture had included that check; nevertheless products were required to conform to Tower standards of weight and fineness, and from the middle of 1643 many royalist coins were marked with abbreviated mint-names to distinguish their origins. Despite obvious temptation, efforts clearly were made to maintain the stipulated standards, and significant debasement appears occasionally only late in the war, notably in the Cary series in the West. However, the fineness of articles of plate will have varied somewhat, making adhesion to the standards harder to achieve. Some silver was so poor that at Oxford Sir William Parkhurst was obliged to refine it before coining, while Thomas Bushell was able to use his highly-refined Welsh silver to improve the quality of mixed melts at Shrewsbury, Oxford (during the early period) and Bristol. Oxford's gold shows a progressive decline to around 20 carats fine. It is harder to be sure about the maintenance of weight standards because of the contemporary prevalence of clipping and the culling of overweight specimens. Discounting clipped coins, surviving royalist issues appear to be comparable with Tower coins, though at York (the only case studied in detail) weights seem to fall about five per cent short of standard. This may relate to the experimental nature of the machinery used there, but could hint at a deliberate eking out of limited bullion, seen in a more blatant way in the emergency ('siege') coinage of Carlisle (pp. 74–5).

The bulk of all business, on both sides, employed the Tower Mint money already in circulation. The output of the royalist mints was by contrast feeble, but usefully supplemented Tower coin in local transactions. Oxford's output went to the Treasurer at War, John Ashburnham; Vyvyan was required successively to deliver coin to Sir Ralph Hopton (1642), Hugh Hodges, Deputy Treasurer of the western army (November 1643) and Sir John Berkeley, Governor of Exeter (January 1643/4), while the products of Cary's mints went to Prince Rupert or his deputies. A recent find from North Yorkshire (Breckenbrough) included York coins in a hoard which may be related to the regular purchasing of provisions for the York garrison and Oxford issues accounted for one-fifth of a small hoard buried at Old Marston, just outside that city. Thus, the localized occurrence of royalist coins as attested by the wartime hoards can help to suggest the origins of those coins whose mints are not explicitly identified. For the most part, surviving coins may be attributed to the known mints. They are either marked, or fall into clear groups which can be related to securely-identified types. The larger mints produced a range of denominations including, occasionally, gold; it appears that there were also several smaller mints, whose output was restricted to halfcrowns (see Table III). Few of their sites can be identified and the rarity of their products hints at tiny outputs based on collected plate. They may have operated at local tax-collecting centres as branches of the authorized mints, each equipped with a simple coining machine whose operation required no great skill, as is evident from their products.

The late stages of the war saw a succession of sieges as isolated royalist garrisons were reduced. In some, there was little need for money, but at Carlisle, Scarborough and Newark emergency money was issued by authority of the Governor. These coinages were purely local and of distinctive designs, as was that of the defenders of Pontefract during its extended siege in 1648−48/9. Meanwhile the mint-cities themselves were isolated and taken, beginning with York in July 1644. The tiny output, compared with the uninterrupted flood of Tower coin, has been mentioned. The royalist mints, even Oxford the biggest, were of so small account that none is mentioned in any articles of surrender. However, attempts were made to seize minting materials and lists survive of tools and dies surrendered at Exeter in 1646 and at the Silver Mills (Dyfi-Furnace), the post-war revival of Aberystwyth, in 1648/9. On 14 July 1646, three weeks after Oxford's surrender, the Commons ordered that 'Trunks lately come from Oxon' be searched for materials belonging to the mint, to be seized and reported to the House for disposal.

Chapter 3

The King's Mint

The value of a provincial mint with a loyal master may have been foreseen by Charles I when he authorized its establishment. Aberystwyth's last delivery of coined money was entered in Bushell's account book on 20 September 1642. The furnaces were drawn and the mint was on the move, summoned to Shrewsbury by the King to coin the plate that he hoped his supporters would provide. The following year was to see two more transfers for Bushell: to Oxford, which became the King's main mint, and then to Bristol where until August 1645 he ran the branch mint set up after the royalist capture of that city. The distinctive products of these 'Royal' mints of the Civil War will be described in the order in which the mints were established.

 Shrewsbury mint

In this same town of Sirosberi his Majesty has set them to work these last days in melting down old silver plate ... He has had all this coined into money to supply the pay of the army and the other expenses required.

Upon receipt of the King's summons, Thomas Bushell closed the Aberystwyth mint and moved its equipment and staff to Shrewsbury, probably arriving around the end of the month − on the 28th, the King, speaking of having 'sent hither for a mint', still awaited it. Bushell may have been joined there by Sir William Parkhurst, Warden of the Tower Mint. Work presumably started at the beginning of October, perhaps in the castle (**34**), though our earliest reference comes in a letter from the Venetian ambassador in London, Giovanni Giustinian, quoted above, which was written on 14 October. According to a Shrewsbury resident writing on the 18th 'the mint is come to our town, and one Master Bushell doth coin every day, for abundance of plate is sent unto the King from the several counties about us ...'.

Although the mint had brought some of its dies with it (**38, 39**), it faced for the first time the necessity of making its own − an opportunity for improvisation which was seized enthusiastically to give us the most characteristic royalist coinage of the war, known to contemporaries as 'Exurgat money' (**35−37**). In place of the royal arms, the King's aims as declared at Wellington on 19th September were set out in Latin abbreviated form: RELIG:PROT:LEG:ANGL:LIBER:PAR ('The

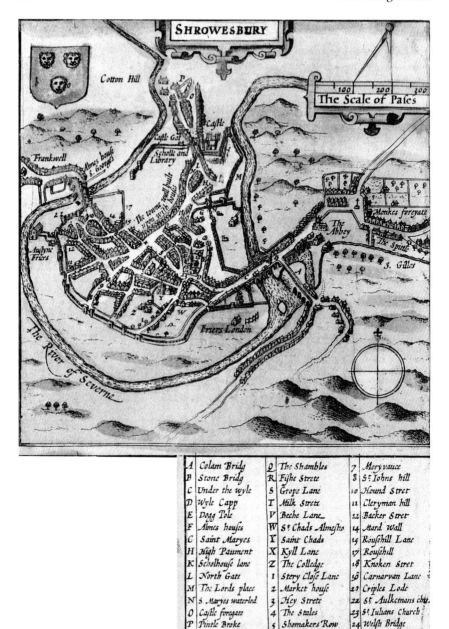

A	Colam Bridg	Q	The Shambles	7	Meryvauce
B	Stone Bridg	R	Fishe Strete	8	S? Iohns hill
C	Under the wyle	S	Grope Lane	10	Hound Strete
D	Wyle Capp	T	Milk Strete	11	Cleryman hill
E	Dogg Tole	V	Beche Lane	12	Backer Stret
F	Almes houses	W	S? Chads Almesho	14	Mard Wall
G	Saint Maryes	Y	Saint Chads	15	Roushill Lane
H	High Paument	X	Kyll Lane	17	Roushill
K	Scholhouse lane	Z	The Colledge	18	Knoken Stret
L	North Gate	1	Stery Close Lane	19	Carnarvan Lane
M	The Lords place	2	Market house	21	Criples Lode
N	S. Maryes waterlod	3	Hey Strete	22	S? Aulkemans chu.
O	Castle foregate	4	The Stales	23	S? Iulians Church
P	Tintle Broke	5	Shomakers Row	24	Welsh Bridge

Fig. 34 Shrewsbury, viewed from the south. A vignette from Speed's map of Shropshire (1616), showing the town's position within a loop of the river Severn, guarded by the castle on its landward side. *British Library.*

Fig. 35 Silver twenty shillings, Shrewsbury 1642. The largest silver type ever struck in England, this 'medal' weighs about 120 grammes, or nearly 4 Troy ounces. The equestrian portrait is made from the same punch as that of the silver crown, **24**, purloined from the Tower. The reverse die was used again at Oxford (see **42**).

Protestant Religion, the laws of England, the liberty of Parliament'), surrounded by verse 1 of Psalm 68: EXVRGAT DEVS DISSIPENTVR INIMICI ('Let God arise, let his enemies be scattered'), a Vulgate tag familiar on the early coinage of James I. Welsh feathers, the date (unusual on contemporary English coinage) and on many dies (**35, 36**) the value fill out a distinctive propagandist design which was soon known even in London, where as early as 21 October the Venetian ambassador referred to the new mottoes and their implied message in a further letter to the Doge and Senate:

> Upon the money coined at Sirosberi the King has had another motto printed instead of the usual inscription, to wit Exurgat Deus

Fig. 36 Silver ten shillings, Shrewsbury 1642, showing the locally-engraved 'Shrewsbury horseman'.

Fig. 37 Halfcrown, Shrewsbury 1642.

Fig. 38 Halfcrown, Shrewsbury, undated (1642); struck using a reverse die from Aberystwyth.

Fig. 39 Shilling, Shrewsbury 1642. Only a few shillings were struck at Shrewsbury, mostly using an Aberystwyth die, as here; another shilling die, bearing a very crude portrait, was engraved locally.

et Dissipentur inimici ejus, and another in the middle Pro Religione et Parliamento [*sic*], all in order to make it more and more patent to his people that his intentions are directed solely to the preservation of religion and the privileges of the country and remote from those ambitious designs which for their own purposes are put abroad by those who have been the authors of the plan to bring a prince of such blameless habits to a state so deplorable.

The message of the new royal coins was clearly understood.

At about the same time, Bushell distributed around £2,000 worth of the new money to the royal army '. . . to each Collonell, the medall of a 20s piece of silver, all the other Officers ten or five, and each Private Soldier Half a Crown', as an advance of pay a few days before Edgehill. These 'medalls' may be identified with the massive silver denominations of the Exurgat money (**35, 36**). They may have been produced because of a shortage of gold for the normal ten- and twenty-shilling pieces, but the name 'medall' also no doubt circumvented Bushell's lack of authority to strike *coins* larger than a halfcrown.

After the inconclusive battle of Edgehill on 23 October (both sides claimed a victory, though the Parliament retired from the field) the mint remained at Shrewsbury until December, when it was ordered to Oxford, which in the meantime had become the King's wartime headquarters.

 **Oxford mint**

Bushell's mint left Shrewsbury late in December 1642 and arrived at Oxford on Tuesday, 3 January 1642/3, as part of a convoy which included a supply of Welsh silver ore. It was installed at New Inn Hall (**40**), the site now of St Peter's College, which, deserted by its Puritan inhabitants, had been requisitioned for this purpose in mid-December. The King lost no time in seeking more raw materials. On 6 January he wrote to all colleges demanding that they lend him 'all such plate of what kind soever' belonging to them, 'promising you to see the same justly repayed unto you after the rate of 5s the ounce for white, and 5s 6d for gilt plate.' Receipts were issued, signed by Parkhurst and Bushell, the 'officers of our mint'. Twelve colleges complied, with contributions ranging from 41 lb (Balliol) to 296 lb (Magdalen). Only Exeter and St John's demurred, but they too were eventually forced to deliver. St John's, thinking thereby to save its plate, sent its equivalent value in money, but the King was not deflected. He kept the money, sent a second time to demand the plate and had it, 224 lb 4 oz in all.

Exeter fought hard to save its plate. To the King's letter of 6 January, the College replied with a petition to the effect that to hand over the plate, upon any pretext whatsoever, would be contrary to its statutes. On 28 January the King replied through the Master of Requests, Sir Thomas Aylesbury, reiterating his claims on the college's loyalty, to which the following submission was returned:

> The Rector and ffellowes of Exeter Colledge uppon serious con-
> sideration of his Majestie's gratious Answere to their humble

Fig. 40 New Inn Hall, Oxford, from Loggan's *Oxonia Illustrata*, 1677. *Society of Antiquaries of London.*

petition are ready to satisfy his desire & obey his commands concerninge their plate expressed in his Royal letters of the 6th of Jan 1642. But with these humble desires, wch they trust his Majesty will bee pleased gratiously to assent to.

1. That in regard of the greate quantity of plate wch they are to part withall & ye poverty of their Colledge, a debt of 138^l, wch they have incurred by means of their late loane to his Majesty may be satisfied out of ye money arising fro⁻ their plate, & that his Majesty would bee pleased to graunte a Warrant that it may be taken up out ye Mint now in Oxford.
2. That a Reservation bee made of their Comunion Plate, wch they are p'suaded his Majesty intends not to make use of.
3. That some time bee allowed them for taking out ye names & titles of the severall Donors, together with ye weight of the severall pieces, that so their memories, as they well deserved, may be p'served to Posterity.

On the 30th the King conceded the last two requests — 'His majesty is well contented that a reservation be made of their Communion plate, which his Majesty never expected upon his former letter' — but would not budge on the debt:

> ... But his Ma^{ty} hopes, shortly to be able to make a full repayment both for this plate, and the money formerly lent Him, that soe the College may not only pay the debt of £138 owing by them, but have their Treasury repaired, besides the conscience of have so seasonably served and supplied his Ma^{ty}.

Three days later the plate, duly recorded in *A Register of severall peeces of Plate lent to the King ffeb: 2.1642. towards the supply of his Majestie's extraordinary necessity at that time*, was handed over.

No fewer than four of Charles I's mintmasters were involved, however indirectly, in the story of Exeter College's plate. Bushell and Parkhurst signed for it (**41**), melted it and coined it. Sir Thomas Aylesbury, Master of Requests and joint master of the Tower Mint, had been ejected by Parliament in 1642; he followed the King to Oxford, where he continued to hold the Court of Requests. (He was to die in comparative poverty in Breda in 1657, aged 81). And the fourth? Among the many entries in the *Register*, which survives, we may note in passing a tankard of white plate weighing 28 oz 1 dwt which bore the following inscription:

> Ex dono Richardi Vyvian — ffrancisci Vyvian Equitis
> Aurati fillii natu maximi, et hujus Collegii Commensalis 1628

— enough silver to pay a cavalryman for nearly two months, could the future Truro-Exeter mintmaster have but known.

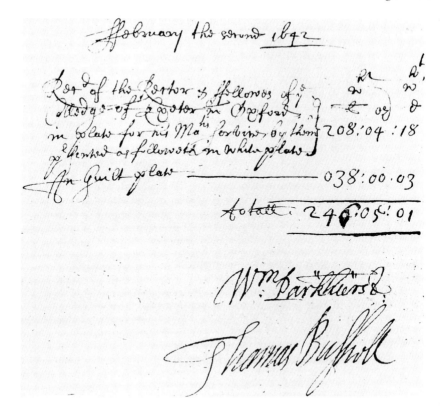

Fig. 41 Oxford plate: receipt signed by Parkhurst and Bushell, 2 February 1642/3, for 246 lb of white and gilt plate surrendered reluctantly by Exeter College 'for his Majesty's service'. *Exeter College, Oxford.*

Apart from chapel plate, little was excepted. An ostrich egg mounted in silver-gilt belonging to Exeter College was spared, for instance, presumably on account of its small value, while one notable survivor is the 42-ounce 'Founder's Cup' belonging to Magdalen College. This silver-gilt covered cup, made *c.* 1601–3, but surmounted by a figure of St Mary Magdalene which had perhaps come from a vessel of the time of the founder, William Wayneflete (d. 1486), was saved at the last moment when Dr Accepted Frewen, the College's President, bought it back from Sir William Parkhurst for its full value, £11 11s 6d. Frewen probably removed it from Oxford in 1644 when appointed Bishop of Lichfield, and was able to return it to the College after the Restoration.

So, by early February 1642/3, plate to the value of about £8,500 (2,782 lb 9 oz 8 dwt, including contributions from the gentry and clergy), plus unknown amounts from four other colleges and the Oxford Halls, had reached the mint. This and the £100 or so per week of Welsh silver received until the late summer presumably formed the bulk of the £13,188 14s 6d received 'from your Majesty's Mynt at divers payments' by the Treasurer at War, John Ashburnham, between November 1642 and October 1643. Total output was probably higher, since Ashburnham accounts separately for £640-worth of silver plate, such as the three dozen trenchers worth £89 from Lady Horwood, and a gold chain valued at £105 (about 2½ lb weight) looted from a prominent parliamentarian, Sir John Wilde. Other contributions included plate, since Ashburnham occasionally had to make up the losses in coining its variable quality, but we have no means of quantifying these. It is certain, though, that estimates suggesting that Oxford's output was measured in hundreds of thousands of pounds are wild exaggerations.

In the late summer of 1643, Thomas Bushell was sent to Bristol to set up a branch mint, leaving Parkhurst in charge at Oxford. Other members of the Oxford staff may be identified: Richard Nicholls, who served at Shrewsbury, Oxford and Bristol; and Robert Hunt, originally seconded to Aberystwyth, who died in Oxford on 9 October 1643. Oxford also saw the emergence of the talents of Thomas Rawlins, playwright and sometime pupil of Nicholas Briot, who was appointed Graver of Seals, Stamps and Medals in 1643 and (nominally) chief graver in the Tower of London and elsewhere in England and Wales in April 1645, no doubt in response to Parliament's promotion of Thomas Simon and Edward Wade. Rawlins' most famous work is the

Fig. 42 Silver twenty shillings, Oxford, dated 1642. The equestrian obverse by Rawlins is one of the finest pieces of English die-engraving of the period. See **35** for the earlier use of the reverse die at Shrewsbury.

1644 Crown (**51** and **Colour Plate VI**); but he was also responsible
inter alia for the obverse die of the 'fine work' silver twenty shillings
dated 1642 (**42**), a portrait medal of Sir William Parkhurst (**52**) and the
elegant gold coinage of 1644 (**Colour Plate IV**).

Since the new year was reckoned from Lady Day (25 March) the
early Oxford products, like those of Shrewsbury, bore the date 1642.
Telling the two apart can be difficult, but is conventionally achieved by
noting the form of the 'Welsh feathers' which on virtually all Oxford
coins marked OX and dated 1643 and later (e.g., **50**) bear labels or
'bands' for the Prince of Wales's motto (though it is not expressed
because of the small scale). Those coins dated 1642 with this form of
the badge are therefore regarded as Oxford products and the others
without bands are ascribed to Shrewsbury; the section headings in this
chapter demonstrate these differences. This distinction is broadly correct, but some of Shrewsbury's dies continued in use at Oxford to start
with, if indeed they were not made at Oxford to the same pattern, as a
gold £3 piece may suggest (see below).

Fig. 43 Gold £3 piece, Oxford, dated 1642. An imposing, if
inartistic creation, and by far the largest English denomination of the time. The King's sword and olive branch
offer a symbolic choice between war and peace.

Oxford was the only royalist mint to coin significant amounts of
gold, the raw material coming from jewellery and personal ornaments
such as Sir John Wilde's gold chain. Twenty- and ten-shilling pieces
matched contemporary Tower standards, but the propaganda value of
royal gifts was not neglected. In February 1642/3 a magnificent £3
piece was introduced (**43**) and the message of the King's 'new coin'
spread by a specially-printed pamphlet which included ink impressions
of its dies. (One pair of dies bears 'Shrewsbury' feathers, all of the
others the Oxford form.) In silver there was a full range of denominations
from the penny up to the great silver coins of twenty shillings (e.g. **44,
45, 54**). However, the characteristic denomination, here as elsewhere,

Fig. 44 Silver crown, Oxford 1643, with a new equestrian effigy usually described today as the 'Oxford horseman'.

Fig. 46 Sixpence, Oxford 1643, using an Aberystwyth obverse die.

was the halfcrown (**50, 55**). All but some of the smallest coins are normally of the 'Exurgat' type and some of the smaller denominations, which were not struck at Shrewsbury, were produced using dies brought from Aberystwyth (**46, 54**).

The mint was also responsible for the production of medals for presentation to the King's supporters, which usually take the form of oval badges of silver or silver-gilt, bearing the King's portrait (**53**). In May 1643 Parkhurst and Bushell were instructed (**47**) to produce special silver badges to be awarded on the recommendation of their commanders to those soldiers 'who have done us faithful service in the Forlorne-Hope' (which consisted of volunteers or picked troops who

CHARLES R.   **CHARLES P.**

RUSTY and well-beloved We greet you well. Whereas We have received information that those Souldiers which have been forward to serve Us in the Forlorn hope, are not looked upon according to their merited Valour and Loyall service. We doe therefore require, that from hence-forward the Commanders in chiefe, both of Horse and Foot, which lead up the Forlorne-hope, upon whom also We mean to bestow speciall tokens of Our Princely favour, doe signify in writing the names of those souldiers whom they find most forward in serving Us their King, and Country, that care may be taken to reward their deservings, and make them specially known to all Our good Subjects; For which end we have thought fit to require Sir *William Parkhurst*, Knight, and *Thomas Bushell*, Esquire, Wardens of Our Mint, to provide from time to time certain Badges of Silver, containing Our Royall Image, and that of Our dearest sonne Prince *Charles*, to be delivered to weare on the breast of every man who shall be certified under the hands of their Commanders in chiefe to have done us faithfull service in the Forlorne-hope. And we doe therefore most straitly command, That no Souldier at any time doe sell, nor any of Our Subjects presume to buy or weare any of these said Badges, other then they, to whom we shall give the same; and that under such paine and punishment as Our Councell of Warre shall think fit to inflict, if any shall presume to offend against this Our Royall command. And We farther require the said Commanders, and Wardens of Our Mint, to keep severall Registers of the names of those, and of their Country, for whom they shall give their Certificates. *Given at Our Court at* OXFORD, *the Eighteenth day of* May. **1643.**

To Our Trusty and wellbeloved Sir WILLIAM PARKHURST *Knight, and* THOMAS BUSHELL *Esquire, Wardens of Our Mint at* Oxford.

Fig. 47 Printed warrant for silver badges for the Forlorn Hope, Oxford 18 May 1643. *Ashmolean Museum, Oxford.*

formed a vanguard or other dangerous service unit), an interesting anticipation of the present-day system of military decorations (**48**). The badge was apparently the idea of Thomas Bushell, who also provided the silver for making it. The die was also used to make a special gold

Fig. 48 Silver badge for the Forlorn Hope, 1643. This corresponds in almost every detail to the woodcut on the warrant (**47**), with the addition of TR in monogram, for Thomas Rawlins. It has no reverse, since it was designed for wear on the breast, sewn to a sash or to the recipient's tunic (hence the holes in the rim). The octagonal shape may have been intended to distinguish it, as a true military decoration, from other oval royalist badges such as **53**.

medal, commissioned on 1 June 1643, for Sir Robert Welch, who had rescued the King's standard at Edgehill. There are also a few strictly commemorative medals, celebrating events such as the capture of Bristol, and the reunion of the King and Queen on the field of Edgehill near Kineton on 13 July 1643 (**49**).

Fig. 49 Silver medal by Rawlins commemorating the reunion of King Charles I and Queen Henrietta Maria (returned from the Continent via York and Newark) on the field of Edgehill, near Kineton, Warwickshire, 13 July 1643. The meeting and the 'defeat of the rebels in the West' (at Roundway Down, Wiltshire) on the same day are seen as an omen of victory and peace. *British Museum*.

Fig. 50 Halfcrown, 1644 with signature OX; from the Penybryn hoard. The pose of the horseman on the later Oxford silver resembles that on Briot's experimental issues (e.g. **20**).

Fig. 51 Crown, 1644 OX, by Rawlins. A more accomplished, if less lively horseman than **42**, framing a view of Oxford after the manner of contemporary Continental coins, depicting churches, colleges and the city's fortifications. Sometimes held to be a pattern, the number surviving and the poor production standard of some of them suggest that a substantive issue was intended. *British Museum*.

Fig. 53 Cast silver badge with loop for suspension, by Rawlins, *c.* 1643–5.

Fig. 52 Sir William Parkhurst, by Rawlins, Oxford 1644. The Oxford mint master is holding an oval badge similar to **53**. The National Museum of Wales's specimen consists of a silver 'shell' mounted in the centre of an eighteenth-century pewter dish. Actual diameter = 80mm.

Fig. 54 Threepence, Oxford *c.* 1644, using an Aberystwyth reverse die.

The early months of 1644 may have been busy at the Oxford mint, since in February the King had appealed by letter to selected supporters to contribute towards £100,000 needed for that year's campaign. How much was raised is not known, but surviving receipts suggest that a proportion was paid in plate. Production may have been interrupted in October by a severe fire in Oxford, but the building used for the mint survived. Output in 1645 seems to have been small, but coins dated 1646 (i.e. produced during the three months 25 March to 24 June, when the city surrendered) are surprisingly common (**55**), perhaps because the siege of Oxford and the end of the war restricted their circulation and encouraged their retention as souvenirs.

Fig. 55 Halfcrown, Oxford 1646. Note that the King's head has been deliberately defaced, an act of spite oc-casionally paralleled on coins of other rulers, especially Louis XVI of France.

 **Bristol mint**

The capture of Bristol, then England's second largest city, on 26 July 1643 gave the royalists a much-needed major port and its potential economic importance to them helps to explain the establishment there of a branch mint derived from Oxford, probably by the autumn. Thomas Bushell was sent to Bristol and later claimed to have spent £1,020 repairing the castle and setting up the mint within it. Bushell himself lodged with an apothecary, Mr Edwards, on Bristol Bridge, then lined on both sides with tall houses (**56**). His regular shipments of Welsh silver were until late in 1644 diverted to Bristol *via* Swansea and there may also have been prize goods in the spring of 1645 as well as continuing contributions in plate.

Some early Bristol coins are similar to Oxford's (several Oxford dies were taken to Bristol), but they may be distinguished by the form of the 'Declaration', which is more condensed (RELIG:PROT:LE:AN:LI:

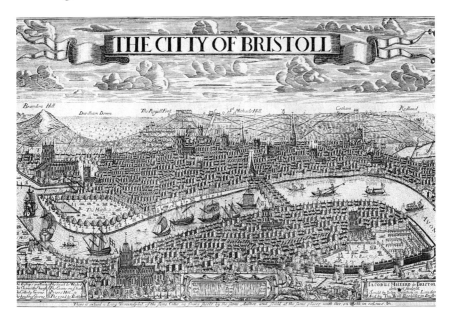

THE CITTY OF BRISTOLL

Fig. 56 Bristol, from the south. The central portion of James Millerd's panoramic view, 1673. The castle had been demolished in 1656, but Bristol Bridge, with its houses, may be seen in the centre. In the foreground are the southern defences, which repulsed both royalist and parliamentarian troops, in 1643 and 1645 respectively. 'Royall Fort' marks the site of the largest of a chain of outworks which protected the city's northern approaches. *City of Bristol Museum and Art Gallery.*

PA:) and the *Exurgat* legend, which here begins at the top of the design (**57**). The 'Bristol feathers' are distinctive too, the label being intertwined with the stems of the ostrich plumes. Bushell's engraver soon evolved a characteristic style and the dies were marked with BR in monogram.

Fig. 57 Halfcrown, Bristol 1643. A typical early Bristol coin, with horseman similar to Oxford (e.g. **44**) and BR monogram on the reverse.

Rudimentary blank preparation and unskilled striking gave halfcrowns of a somewhat rough-and-ready appearance, sometimes squarish in shape (**58**); but the smaller denominations were carefully made (**59– 61; 63**). A former Aberystwyth die was used to strike threepences in 1644 (**60**). Pride of place in the Bristol series belongs to the gold twenty-shilling pieces of 1645 which were probably struck for court use during Prince Charles's stay at Bristol as nominal head of the royalists in the West (**62; Colour Plate V**). At the other extreme, it was reported in the House of Commons in September 1644 that the royalists were making farthing tokens at Bristol, allegedly for troops' pay. Any such issues cannot be distinguished today; the large-scale use of tokens for pay is inherently unlikely, since their currency was strictly limited, to a maximum of sixpence-worth in a transaction of ten shillings, or to one penny in a shilling.

Fig. 58 Halfcrown, Bristol 1644, signed BR in monogram on both sides and unusually well struck.

Figs. 59–61 Bristol, smaller denominations: sixpence, 1644; threepence, 1644; halfgroat, undated. The three-pence is struck from an Aberystwyth obverse die.

Fig. 62 Gold twenty shillings, Bristol 1645. A handsome and carefully made coin for Court use.

Fig. 63 Shilling, Bristol 1645: compare with **64** and **67**.

'Late Declaration' coinage

Bristol surrendered to Fairfax on 11 September 1645, by which time Bushell had probably already retired to Lundy Isle, off the north Devon coast, which he was to hold until the end of the war. His moneyers, however, appear to have continued work until the final months of the war, using altered Bristol dies and others of similar types, perhaps at three locations, since their products are distinguished by the letters A (on coins dated 1645: **64**) or B (1646: **65**), or by a small plume of feathers (also 1646: **66**–**68**).

In keeping with royalist mint practice, these letters and the feathers symbol are likely to denote different mints, and there have been various attempts to identify them. Of possible Welsh mints, Aberystwyth

Fig. 64 Shilling, 1645A. Found at Clywedog, near Dolgellau, Merioneth (now part of Gwynedd), *c.* 1940.

Fig. 65 Sixpence, 1646B.

(where a small coining of silver, otherwise unidentified, was recorded in January 1645/6) and Beaumaris have been suggested; in the West, Appledore and Barnstaple, both in north Devon. By the autumn of 1645 these areas, together with parts of the Midlands and the Welsh Marches, were all that remained in royalist hands. Only three find spots have been recorded for these 'Late Declaration' issues: near Dolgellau (Gwynedd: **64**) and Telford (Shropshire) for 'A' coins and

Figs. 66–68 Halfcrown, shilling and threepence, 1646 'feathers'. The shilling obverse is an altered Bristol die, on which the BR monogram before CAROLVS may still be discerned beneath the 'feathers' mark.

an imprecise location near Pershore, Worcestershire for a shilling of the 'feathers' group. These suggest that a West Country source is unlikely.

George Boon has recently made out a coherent case, based on known movements of royalist troops, for identifying the first two mints as Ashby-de-la-Zouch, in Leicestershire and Bridgnorth, in Shropshire, both important garrisons which survived until late in the war. Minting equipment could well have been conveyed from Bristol to Oxford and thence to Ashby, which received strong reinforcements from Oxford late in September 1645. In turn, when Ashby surrendered on honourable terms on 28 February 1645/6, its garrison had liberty to march away to Bridgnorth or Worcester. Bridgnorth was held until 26 April 1646, which would have given enough time for an issue of coins marked 1646B. On the present evidence, these attributions are entirely reasonable, but the few find spots do not in themselves rule out other places of origin for these enigmatic issues.

Chapter 4

The West: Sir Richard Vyvyan's Mints

The royalist attempt to secure the West Country when war broke out failed utterly, and the Marquess of Hertford and Sir Ralph Hopton were chased out of Somerset and North Dorset. The Marquess escaped across the Bristol Channel to Cardiff; Hopton, with a small body of dragoons and horse, retired to Cornwall. Accused there of disturbing the peace, he stood trial voluntarily at Truro and was acquitted by a packed jury, whereupon Cornwall declared for the King, one of very few counties to do so.

On 14 November 1642, Sir Richard Vyvyan of Trelowarren, MP for Tregony and head of one of Cornwall's oldest landed families (**Colour Plate VII**), was commissioned to coin bullion or plate of gold or silver 'with the dies stampes and forms as the monies now current within Our Realm of England'; and to deliver 'the Bullyon and Plate, so by you coyned . . . to Our trusty Sir Ralph Hopton, Knight of the Bath . . .'. On 19 November, the local royalist leaders urged Vyvyan to 'make your speedy repaire to us', suggesting Bodmin or Liskeard as possible sites for his mint and authorizing him to offer eight per cent on plate lent by supporters. Three of the local gentry were entrusted with procuring staff and tools for the mint.

Truro mint

In the event, the mint was set up at Truro, a Stannary town and port rather nearer Vyvyan's own house, and more secure from the threat of raiding from Devon (**69, 71**). Our evidence for its location comes from one of the first to contribute plate, Jonathan Rashleigh of Menabilly, who took £104-worth to be 'melted for the King's service at Trewroe'; and an undated account, probably of January 1642/3, refers to the costs of carriage of a trunk of plate seized from Lord Robartes of Lanhydrock 'to Trewrow to the Mynt'. Another unwilling contributor to the royalist war effort was a Plymouth merchant, Robert Trelawney, from whom 681 oz of plate and a gold hatband weighing 3 oz were taken by Sir Nicholas Slanning on 14 January 1642/3.

A royalist victory at Braddock Down (19 January 1642/3) was followed by a serious reverse at Modbury, Devon (21 February); and although local truces bought time in February and March, hostilities were soon

Fig. 69 Halfcrown, Truro 1642, privy-mark *Rose*. The obverse design may be an allusion to the King's 'victory' at Edgehill, 23 October 1642; this die was re-used at Exeter in 1644.

Fig. 70 The Scots Rebellion, silver medal, London 1639. An early work by Thomas Simon and probably the source for the design of **69**.

Fig. 71 Halfcrown, undated, Truro 1642–3, p.m. *Rose*. It is sometimes suggested that the unusual T-shaped punctuation marks on the reverse were intended to represent the mint's initial.

resumed. On 10 April 1643, the Cornish royalists met at Bodmin, short of money and threatened with invasion from Parliament-held Devon. They decided to levy a weekly rate of £750 on the county and to raise a voluntary loan of plate. Lists of the plate gathered at Liskeard by 18 April and Killaton by the 24th, formerly at Mount Edgcumbe, near Plymouth, were unfortunately destroyed by an air raid in 1941;

but Hopton's narrative tells us that £3,000-worth was brought in. Hopton's army numbered only 2,400 foot and 500 horse, paid perhaps 8d and 2s 6d per day respectively. The ability to coin even £3,000, though small compared with the output of the Tower Mint, may thus from a regional viewpoint be seen as an important contribution to the royalist campaign in the summer of 1643, since it provided significant help in fielding an army which against all odds defeated a much larger and well-entrenched parliamentary force at Stratton, near Bude, on 16 May. The subsequent campaign was one of the greatest royalist successes of the war, for the entire peninsula was overrun (only Plymouth and Lyme Regis held out against them); it culminated in the battle of Roundway Down, near Devizes, on 13 July (see **49**), the capture of Bristol on 26 July and, finally, that of Exeter on 4 September, whither Vyvyan's mint was soon moved.

Fig. 72 Sir Richard Vyvyan's second commission under the Great Seal, 3 January 1643/4. The text is transcribed in the Appendix on pp. 108−9. *Vyvyan papers, Cornwall Record Office.*

Exeter mint

A branch mint at Exeter had been planned by the Parliament in December 1642, but was probably never opened (see p. 92). Technically, the royalist mint there dates from a commission issued to Vyvyan on 3 January 1643/4, which empowered him to set up one or more mints in the counties of Devon and Cornwall and city of Exeter (72 and Appendix). However, two account books from the mint survive in the Vyvyan papers; they cover the period 27 September 1643 to 2 April 1644 and show that it was set up almost immediately after Exeter was captured. In this time, £1,460 was coined from plate brought in by local people of all persuasions, who were credited with 4s 10d per ounce of touched (hallmarked) gilt plate or 4s 8d for touched white plate (the rates for untouched plate, whose fineness was uncertain, were 4s 2d and 4s 0d), accepted as loans. Copies of all receipts and other documents were kept by the mint's clerk, Thomas Hawkes, the only other member of staff who can be positively identified, though it is sometimes suggested that Samuel Calle (or Cawley), a local goldsmith for whom Vyvyan stood surety as a freeman of the city in 1645, may have been the engraver. The mint itself may have been located at the house belonging to Hannah Anthony which Vyvyan occupied from 1643 to 1646, which perhaps lay in St Olave's parish.

Vyvyan spent most of the war in Exeter, though in January 1643/4 he attended the Oxford Parliament and in August 1644 took part in the King's campaign in Cornwall against the forces of the Earl of Essex. At Boconnoc on 3 September 1644 he was created a baronet for his services to the royal cause, which also included erecting and garrisoning a fort at Dennis Head to guard the Helford river. Exeter was besieged in December 1645 and surrendered on 13 April 1646. There is no Exeter coinage dated 1646, while much of that dated 1645 may well have been produced late in the old-style year, under siege and therefore of restricted circulation. There is only one coin of that year in the late Civil War hoard found in 1895 at East Worlington, 19 miles north of Exeter, which otherwise included a considerable batch of Vyvyan's products, though these formed only one per cent of the 5,188 coins found.

Vyvyan spent the last weeks of the siege in prison, having fallen out with the governor, Sir John Berkeley, for speaking 'civilly' of Fairfax's army. He was comprised within the Exeter articles of surrender, but still faced immense local hostility. His house in Exeter was searched and the mint tools – his personal property valued at £15 – were seized. Quite apart from having to compound for his estates, he also faced a number of lawsuits concerning plate taken to the mint and for unlawfully occupying the Exeter house. Vyvyan was only able to clear these up by a costly, lengthy and resolute action, with powerful help from Sir Thomas Fairfax and other senior Parliamentary figures. Even so, he was not finally clear of litigation until July 1650.

Fig. 73 Penny, Exeter 1644, p.m. *Rose.* Compare with **10**.

Fig. 74 Shilling, Exeter 1645, p.m. *Rose.*

Fig. 75 Crown, Exeter 1645, with privy-marks *Castle* (obv.) and *Ex* (rev.).

The Truro and Exeter coinages form a single group united by the re-use of the relatively small number of obverse dies and the use in common of a rose as privy-mark (**69, 71, 73, 74**); at Exeter two further marks were sometimes used, a castle which perhaps was derived from the city's arms and the signature 'Ex' (**75**). At the head of the series, the fine halfcrowns dated 1642 (**69**) may be ascribed to Truro, together with several related types, while all of those dated 1644 and 1645 come from Exeter. In between, there is a considerable group of undated pieces which can only be described as 'Truro or Exeter'. There are also rare gold twenty-shilling pieces made from the likes of Trelawney's hatband and, at Exeter, small silver denominations from sixpence down to a penny (**73**). Silver crowns (e.g., **75**) are a distinct feature of the series, but apart from the use of crown dies to strike ten-shillings at Truro (only one specimen survives), larger denominations similar to those made at Shrewsbury and Oxford were not produced. Apart from some very rare 1644 and 1645 specimens of Exurgat type, the Truro and Exeter coins are generally close, if somewhat crude, copies of the Tower Mint types, as required by Vyvyan's commission. Somehow appended to this series, perhaps, there exist also a few halfcrowns with a bugle as privy-mark, poorly-struck but otherwise reminiscent of coins of Truro. Their place of minting remains a mystery.

The list of tools taken from Vyvyan in 1646 throws some light on the nature of the mint. They included a box of small puncheons and tools, 'six upper and four under stamps [dies] not cutt,' 23 under stamps and 23 upper stamps: the distinction between them, even for uncut dies, suggests that piles and trussels are indicated. The appearance of the coins themselves and the presence in the list of five small anvils, three pairs of tongs, six pairs of shears and ten hammers confirms that the mint used traditional manual techniques. The 23 'under stamps' in fact represent almost all of the obverse dies used in the entire Truro-Exeter series, while the 23 upper stamps will have been those in use towards the end of the mint's life. In all, many more reverse dies were used than obverses, another good indication of the hammer technique of production.

There was a curious postscript to the West Country coinage. In the last months of the war there was a project to revive a mint at Truro under Col. William Smyth, which seems to have come to nothing. Smyth subsequently seems to have set up a mint on the island of Jersey, the destination of Prince Charles and other senior royalists in June 1646. A contemporary Jersey diarist, Jean Chevalier, recorded that halfcrowns, a few shillings and a good number of 'Jacobus' (gold Unites of James I) were produced.

The halfcrowns were said to bear on one side the King on horseback with a sword in his hand and on the other 'the harp, roses [*plural*], fillets, interlaced crosses, and the other devices on the King's coin'; Chevalier later described the reverse as 'the same design as English coin'. The rather loose association of the words 'Truro' and 'roses' has led writers to seek these coins in the Truro-Exeter series, whose privy-mark was *a rose*, but this seems to be misguided. Perhaps the 'roses' were a misinterpretation of the scrolls of the garniture surrounding the shield on many Carolean halfcrowns.

The Jersey mint soon failed, and appears to have been little better than a counterfeiting operation – why else were coins of James I produced except to profit from their higher exchange rate than Charles's gold? None of its products, described by Sir Edward Hyde as 'adulterate' (i.e. light, base or both), has been identified. The Jersey mint was a far cry from the scrupulous operation of Vyvyan's Truro and Exeter mints.

Fig. 76 William Cavendish, successively Earl, Marquess (1643) and Duke (1665) of Newcastle. Nineteenth-century etching after Van Dyck.

Chapter 5

York Mint

About the end of January [1642/3], the King's Mint began to coin in Sir Henry Jenkins house in the Minster Yard.

York was Charles I's 'second capital', and after being forced to leave London he made his way there, arriving on 19 March 1641/2. Until the middle of August his court was based at York or Beverley, whence he directed operations against the port of Hull. The establishment of a mint at York was being planned long before the outbreak of formal hostilities. Nicholas Briot, the King's engraver, was summoned to York by a letter from Secretary of State Edward Nicholas dated 6 May in connection with some proposals concerning currency standards. A letter of 30 May notes that Briot had fallen ill; it does not press him, but on 21 June, Secretary Nicholas ordered Briot to York forthwith 'et vous avertir qu'avez mener avec vous les Roues et toutes autres sortes d'instruments requis et necessaires pour icy battre de la Monnoye qu S. ma'té aura occasion d'ordonner dez que vous serez arrivé'. Shortly after, arrangements were made for Sir William Parkhurst, Warden of the Mint, to advance Briot the money necessary for his journey. On 15 July, these plans received a severe setback when a ship carrying Briot's equipment and personal baggage was held up off Scarborough by one Captain Stevens, who seized the equipment on the grounds that no authority had been given for its removal. Meanwhile on 7 July, David Ramage, a member of Briot's staff, was paid £85 10s for the provision of 'several instruments for the two Mints at York and Shrewsbury'.

The King meanwhile was touring the north Midlands seeking men and supplies. He despatched a warrant establishing the mint at York, which arrived on the very day that its equipment was taken. This we learn from a letter written the following day from Beverley, which was printed in London four days later:

> FRIDAY [*15 July*] a warrant under His Majestie's Broade Seale came to Yorke for the erecting of a new Mynt there, some commissioners appointed for the same came to view the place, where the old Mynt stood, which is now in Sir William Saviles possession, near the Minster, where it appears money was coyned in Hen. 8. Raigne.

The building referred to is St Leonard's Hospital which had housed a mint in 1546. However, August saw the removal of the Court as

Charles set off to raise his standard at Nottingham and to recruit his army in the Welsh Marches. York became a military backwater with a small garrison, and the need for large sums of money moved elsewhere.

In October William Cavendish, Earl of Newcastle and the wealthiest man in the north (**76**), was commissioned General of all forces to be raised in all parts of the kingdom 'Trent-north' and in many Midlands counties which were at that time in parliamentarian hands. He was also empowered to confer knighthoods and to coin money and print when he saw occasion for it. In December he brought his forces to York, where a contemporary diary bewailed the lack of organization: officers and gentry had to dig into their pockets to provide for the army's upkeep. The mint finally started production in January 1642/3, not in St Leonard's Hospital, but in a building in Minster Yard, which survives today as St William's College and now belongs to the Diocese of York (**77**). Christopher Hildyard's *Antiquities of York City*, first published in 1664, gives us our only reference to the mint in action, quoted above. He also tells us that the King's printers set up their presses there on 24 March 1641/2. All but one of them departed in the autumn of 1642, releasing suitable accommodation for the mint.

Four silver denominations were produced at York: halfcrown (**78, 81**), shilling (**80, 82**), sixpence (**83**) and threepence (**79**). Its coins are unique among Civil War issues for the quality of their die-engraving

Fig. 77 St William's College, otherwise 'Sir Henry Jenkins' house in the Minster Yard', site of the York mint, 1643–4. *Photograph by Michael Doe.*

I King Charles I, equestrian portrait by Van Dyck, *c.* 1638.
Reproduced by courtesy of the Trustees, The National Gallery, London.

II A hoard of silver shillings of Elizabeth I, James I and Charles I buried in the bowl of a Jacobean silver cup. Found in 1984 at Dersingham, Norfolk, it was probably buried in the summer of 1643 at the time of the 'royalist' rising at nearby Kings Lynn. The hoard is now in the Kings Lynn Museum. *Photograph: the British Museum.*

III Oxford, silver twenty shillings, dated 1642. Obverse, engraved by Thomas Rawlins (see 42).

IV Oxford, gold £3 piece, 1644, the last year in which
these coins were struck. *British Museum.*

V Bristol, gold twenty shillings, 1645, obverse (see **62**).

VI Oxford, silver crown, 1644, obverse, by Thomas Rawlins. Note signature 'R' at lower left of the design (see **51**). *British Museum.*

VII Sir Richard Vyvyan, 1644; attributed to William Dobson (1611-46). Dobson, described by Aubrey as 'the most excellent painter that England hath yet bred', lodged in Oxford throughout the war, where he produced many portraits of royalist officials. The sitting for this probably took place during Vyvyan's Oxford visit of January—February 1643/4. *Trelowarren, Cornwall.*

VIII York, halfcrown, 1643-4, obverse, showing the incomparable clarity of a coin produced by rotary methods (see 81).

IX Pontefract besieged, shilling 1648 in the name of Charles II, coupled with a 'lifetime' reverse type of Charles I.

X Oliver Cromwell, miniature on vellum by Samuel
Cooper, 1656. *National Portrait Gallery, London.*

XI Charles II, halfcrown of the 'third hammered
issue', 1661-2. A splendid piece which does rare
justice to Simon's portraiture.

Fig. 78 Halfcrown, York *c.* 1643, p.m. *Lion.* The privy-mark, method of production and find spots identify this type as a York coin. Teething trouble with the cutter punch may explain why many coins of this type were crudely cut from the strip using shears.

Figs. 79–80 York threepence and shilling, *c.* 1643, signed EBOR (*Eboracum*), unknown engraver.

Fig. 81 Halfcrown, York 1643–4, EBOR. The horseman copies Tower halfcrowns of 1641–3 (**125**). The dies are likely to be the work of Nicholas Briot. (Penybryn hoard).

Figs. 82−83 York shilling (EBOR) and sixpence, p.m.
Lion, 1643−4, with characteristic portraits by Briot.

and the perfection of the printed image − an apt term, perhaps, since
they were produced on a rotary press. Strips of silver were prepared
and fed between pairs of steel rollers mounted in a machine like a
mangle operated, if Briot's earlier experiments are a guide, by 'two
strong persons'. Each roller bore a series of engraved dies (five or six
for halfcrowns, shillings and sixpences, nine for the threepences) and
the coins were punched out afterwards, a process which could leave a
burred edge on the reverse of the coin (e.g., **80**), which in extreme
cases was filed flat. Almost all York coins are identified by the mint-
signature EBOR (Eboracum, the Latin name for the city) and all use a
lion, an element of the city's arms, as privy mark (**Colour Plate VIII**).

   There also exist several types of 'York' halfcrowns which do not fit
into this scheme. One issue comprises two 'York' types and two which
copy Tower issues of 1639−41, using dies made from a single set of
punches. All are highly debased (as low as 44% silver) using as alloy
copper whitened with arsenic, a standard counterfeiting method, and
are of very low weight, giving intrinsic values around tenpence, i.e.
one-third of their face value. Nowhere did the royalists debase by this
much. An example of a 'Tower' type in the Breckenbrough hoard
shows them to be contemporary, and the coins are well made, but it is
hard to think of them other than as counterfeits. Another small group
of lightweight halfcrowns copies York types, but in good silver. It is
also contemporary, but its status remains uncertain.

   Of course, Newcastle will have delegated the day-to-day running of
the York mint; but there is no written evidence for the names of any of
its officials. Experienced staff may possibly have been recruited from
Edinburgh, where Briot's machines were in use. The active involvement

of Nicholas Briot at York is testified by his correspondence of 1642, his widow's petition to Charles II ('he from time to time did go to York'), the use of rotary coining machinery and the engraving of some of the dies (**82, 83**). His pupil, David Ramage, a competent if uninspired engraver, may have been responsible for the dies for the first group of halfcrowns (e.g., **78**), and we may note that the portraits on the three-pences (**79**) and on one group of shillings (**80**), which were probably early products, lack Briot's refinement and may be by another, un-identified engraver.

The mint's potential importance to the royalists lay not only in converting plate, but also in the recoinage of foreign specie. Until Bristol was captured, the north-eastern ports were a vital channel of supplies from Europe. On 7 March 1642/3, for instance, the Queen arrived at York from the Netherlands bringing supplies rumoured to include large amounts of coin. York's products were used locally, for instance in purchasing foodstuffs. They have been recorded in at least eight hoards from Yorkshire and neighbouring counties, notably those from Breckenbrough, near Thirsk, discovered in 1985, and Pocklington, east of York, found in 1849. The mint probably remained active until the spring of 1644, when York was besieged by the joint armies of Lord Fairfax, the Scots and the Eastern Association. The siege was raised by Prince Rupert on 1 July, but the royalist disaster at Marston Moor the following day led swiftly to a renewed siege which a much-reduced garrison was unable to withstand. Articles for the city's surrender were agreed on 15 July 1644.

Chapter 6

Sir Thomas Cary's Mints

W.H. Black's *Docquets of Letters Patent and Other Instruments passed under the Great Seal of King Charles I at Oxford*, published in 1887, includes on p. 211 the following entry (22 May 1644):

> A commission directed to Sr Thomas Cary K^t whereby his Ma^{ty} doth authorize him to erect one or more Mynts wthin the Counties of Hereford Worcester Salop and Chester and to Coyne moneyes in such manner as in the Tower of London, And to receive for his Paynes and chardges in coyning the said Moneyes such Allowances as are paid in the said Tower of London wthout Accompt and to paie soe much of the said Moneys as shalbe made of the Ingott Bullion or Plate delivered to his Ma^{ts} use, to Prince Rupert or such as he shall appointe.

Sir Thomas 'Cary' is the most shadowy of the royalist mintmasters, and the task of identifying him is not helped by the profusion of Thomas Car(e)ys and Thomas Carews who lived during Charles I's reign. One, the younger brother of the second Earl of Monmouth, is the Thomas Cary, Gentleman of the King's Bedchamber, depicted on a medal by the French engraver Warin in 1633. It has been stated, erroneously, that he served the King during the Civil War and died late in Old-Style 1648; in fact he died (seemingly of consumption) as ambassador-designate to Venice, in April 1634, and must therefore be ruled out as a royalist mintmaster. The only recorded *knight* of this name living in 1644 was the second son of Walter Cary, of Wickham, Bedfordshire, who had been dubbed in Ireland on 10 June 1628.

The commission to supply the Border counties with mints seems at first to be an afterthought, but we know that there had been plans to reopen the Shrewsbury mint in the summer of 1643, which had been shelved after the capture of Bristol. The new franchise perhaps resulted from a combination of administrative reform in the area and a changing military situation in which a network of local mints was seen to be desirable. Mints are known to have existed at Chester and at Hereford, but surviving coins can be securely attributed only to the former. A document giving details of 277 ounces of plate coined at Hereford by 'Rude the coyner' in October–November 1644 was published in 1898 but cannot now be found. The date and place together suggest that one of Cary's mints is concerned. No other mints or coins can be attributed with certainty, but there is a considerable series of coins which represents one or more major royalist mints, together with several small issues of halfcrowns, which appear only in hoards buried in 1644 or later, and whose few recorded find spots indicate origins in the Welsh Marches rather than south-west England, the other main area to which the royalists became increasingly restricted in the later stages of the war. These coins are likely to be products of Cary's mints. If the attributions that follow are correct (and it should be remembered that apart from Chester, they are only suggestions), it would appear that at least one mint was established in each of the four counties.

Chester mint

Chester was garrisoned for the King from September 1642 and remained in royalist hands almost to the end, surrendering only on 3 February 1645/6. It is possible that a mint may have operated there as early as December 1643, but the evidence is inconclusive. The Mayor and Aldermen of the city offered 400 oz of gilt plate (about £100 worth) to Arthur, Lord Capel, as a bribe for the removal of the newly-arrived troops from Ireland. Capel's receipt of 7 December refers to the plate as an 'advance or contribution to the pay and provision of and for the fforces arrived from Ireland and now in his Maties service in thes partes', but we do not know whether it was coined locally; on 16 December the same quantity was signed for, on the same receipt, by a local man, Brian Pretious, and its ultimate fate is unknown. The survival of the plate for at least nine days might argue that no mint yet existed, but Pretious's signature may have been a formality. A mint was certainly working by 31 January 1644/5, when it was ordered that £100-worth of the city's remaining plate be 'fourthwith converted into coyne' towards the city's defence and payment of its debts. One securely-identified Chester halfcrown (**84**) bears the date 1644, i.e. it was struck before 25 March 1645.

Fig. 84 Halfcrown of *Exurgat* type, Chester 1644, privy-marks *Three gerbs and a sword* (obv.), *Feathers* (rev.).

Fig. 85 Chester halfcrown, undated, with p.m.'s *Three gerbs and a sword*, signed CHST. From the same obverse die as **84**, crudely recut with the addition of feathers and the mint signature.

Two types of halfcrown bear as privy-marks the ancient armorials of the city, three gerbs (wheatsheaves) together with the upright sword granted as the crest of the city's new arms in 1580, best seen here on **85**, which is also signed CHST. An exceedingly rare gold twenty shillings (**86**) is linked to this by the use of the same punches in preparing its dies and so should be ascribed to Chester. It was formerly thought to have been produced at Aberystwyth, even though coining in gold lay outside the terms of Bushell's indentures.

Two further types, a halfcrown and a threepence, bear a single prostrate gerb as privy-mark (**87, 88**). All of these coins are linked by their mode of manufacture using a rotary (rocker) press, but apart from the dated type, their chronology is uncertain. There are related shillings and halfcrowns made by this method (e.g., **89, 90**) which are also probably products of Chester or a mint derived from it.

Fig. 86 Gold twenty shillings, undated, p.m. *Feathers*. Attributed to Chester by the identity of the feathers and other punches with those used for the dies of **84** and **85**.

Figs. 87–88 Halfcrown and threepence, with p.m.'s *A single gerb*, probably struck at Chester. The reverse of the halfcrown is similar to the York coins **81–82**.

Fig. 89 Halfcrown with p.m.'s ⋮ and ∴, from the Penybryn hoard. The findspot, only 15 miles away, and similarity to **87** point to a Chester origin.

Fig. 90 Shilling, uncertain mint (Chester?), p.m. ∴

'Worcester' and related issues

The largest of the 'Cary' groups consists of an extensive series of halfcrowns bearing a variety of privy-marks and linked by the use of common punches and dies (**91, 93, 94**); a series of related smaller denominations, from shillings down to halfgroats (**92, 95**); and some very rare twenty-shilling pieces. Apart from a halfcrown of *Exurgat* type dated 1644 whose reverse die was first used at Bristol in 1643 and which heads the sequence, all types bear designs related to Tower Mint issues, as required by Cary's commission.

The first two halfcrown obverse dies of this series bear the letter W beneath the King's horse and in keeping with royalist practice after 1643 this is likely to identify their place of minting, however obscurely (**91**). For many years these were attributed, with reference to the far from specific armorial charges used as privy-marks, to Weymouth, but there is no record of any grant for a Dorset mint and no appropriate finds are recorded from that area. Indeed, as George Boon has pointed out, the royalist ordnance agent in Weymouth, Captain Strachan, was forever complaining about shortage of cash. On the other hand, a West Midlands origin is suggested by finds from Clwyd, Shropshire and the Cotswolds, while some shillings bear a privy-mark resembling a pear (**92**), an element of the arms of Worcester, which held out for the King until 23 July 1646 and seems likely to have been the site of Sir Thomas Cary's principal mint.

Fig. 91 Halfcrown, signed W (Worcester?), with p.m.'s *Castle* (illegible) and *Helmet, c.* 1644−5. From the Penybryn hoard.

Another halfcrown die bears the letters SA and it has been suggested that these signify *Salopia*, the Latin name for Shrewsbury (**93**). In July 1643 Thomas Bushell's plans to reopen the mint there had progressed as far as sending men to prepare the furnaces, so this type may represent an issue at Shrewsbury as one of Cary's mints between May 1644 and 22 February 1644/5, when the town was surprised and captured. The only findspot for an SA halfcrown is apparently Haverfordwest, Dyfed (Pembrokeshire). The SA die was used again (during 1645?) with these letters obliterated by a roundel (the 'cannon ball'

Fig. 92 Shilling, with p.m. *Pear* (?) on the reverse: Worcester or related mint, *c.* 1644–5.

Fig. 93 Halfcrown, signed SA (Salopia?), with p.m.'s *Fleur-de-Lys* and *Scallop, c.* 1644–5. Apparently found at Haverfordwest, Pembrokeshire, *c.* 1954.

mark), presumably at another site (**94**). Halfcrowns from this and later dies in the sequence have been found in Shropshire and Clwyd, while a threepence of related type has recently been found in the Vale of Glamorgan. The coins at the very end of the sequence are noticeably debased, to judge from their appearance, and the few analyses confirm this.

Fig. 94 Halfcrown, 'Salopia' obverse die with signature obliterated ('cannon ball'). Uncertain mint, *c.* 1645.

Fig. 95 Threepence, p.m. *Fleur-de-Lys.* From the W or SA groups of issues, *c.* 1644–5.

'Hartlebury Castle' and other unattributed types

Hartlebury Castle, residence of the Bishop of Worcester, lies about ten miles north of Worcester and in 1644−6, like Worcester, was the site of one of the collection-centres for local taxes, the 'contribution'. There is a group of halfcrowns, all from a single pair of dies, whose privy marks (one and three pears) leave little doubt of a Worcestershire origin (**96**). Hidden in the lower part of the garniture of the reverse shield are the letters HC, and, if these identify the mint, the suggestion of Hartlebury Castle is almost certainly correct. Specimens have occurred in hoards of 1644−6 in the Cotswolds and Shropshire, while an isolated example was found at Hanbury in Worcestershire. Hartlebury Castle was held by the royalists until 16 May 1646. A third Worcestershire centre for collection of the 'contribution' was at Evesham, lost on 26 May 1645. A late nineteenth-century reference to a tradition of a Civil War mint there is suggestive in this context, but there is apparently no evidence that coins were ever struck there, and no coins are suitably marked.

The 'Hartlebury' coins were produced on a simple rotary (rocker) press and there are two other unattributed halfcrown issues which seem to have been made in the same way. The first (**97**) is dated 1644 and bears the initials CH; four specimens only are known to survive and the only recorded findspot is Penybryn, near Wrexham. The second (**98**), also dated 1644, is of *Exurgat* type copying a Bristol original; one may have been included in the 'Cotswolds' hoard buried in 1645. Their crude appearance notwithstanding, both are issues of good silver and weight, and should be regarded as official royalist issues from the Welsh Marches.

The final halfcrown (**99**) in this section is a puzzle. A competent, if unremarkable equestrian obverse is coupled with a reverse of vigour and originality on which the royal arms are surrounded by the Garter and supported by a lion and a unicorn. One specimen, in the British

Fig. 96 Halfcrown, p.m.'s *One* and *Three pears*, signed HC in the garniture of the reverse shield, probably Hartlebury Castle, 1644−6.

Museum, is undated, but all others bear the date 1645. The (unique?) undated coin is of fine silver, but the 1645 coins are all somewhat debased (analyses suggest only about 70−75% silver), a feature shared with some of the latest of the W/SA group discussed above and unusual elsewhere in the royalist coinages. Elias Ashmole, in his *History of the Garter* published in 1672 described the type as stamped in the West of England. He had served the royalists as a Commissioner of the Excise in various places, including Worcester, so it is likely that this curious issue also belongs to this region.

Fig. 97 Halfcrown, 1644 CH (Hereford?), from the Peny-bryn hoard. The date, barely legible at the top of the reverse, is confirmed by the other surviving examples.

Fig. 98 Halfcrown of *Exurgat* type, uncertain mint, 1644. The 'Declaration' follows the form used on Bristol coins from 1643, which suggests a western origin for this type.

Fig. 99 Halfcrown, p.m. *Fleur-de-Lys*, uncertain mint, 1645; reverse, arms with Garter, crown and supporters.

Chapter 7

Foreign Coin

In the normal course of events, any foreign coins entering the country were sent to the Mint for recoining. They were rigorously excluded from circulation, except in certain special circumstances (see p. 8), though Low Countries coins were familiar sights in the East Anglian ports. The war years seem to have seen a considerable increase in the amounts of foreign coinage circulating in England and Wales. A document of 1644 refers to the foreign money in Kent, Sussex, Hampshire and the west of England, while the evidence of modern finds points to significant amounts of coinage from the Low Countries circulating (or at least available for hoarding) in the north and east of England. Although Civil War deposits account for the overwhelming majority of seventeenth-century hoards, the lack of European coins in almost all others of the Stuart period suggests that this increase in foreign coin in England was indeed a wartime phenomenon.

One special cause for this may have been royalist fund-raising on the Continent, especially the Queen's activities in the Low Countries. On 23 February 1641/2 Henrietta Maria left Dover for the Continent, to raise money for the King by pledging her own and some of the Crown Jewels. The high interest charged (12%) was met from profits on the sale of Cornish tin in French and Flemish ports. Much of the borrowed money went to buy arms and equipment, but some arrived in England as specie. Early in the war Thomas Bushell bore the cost of converting 'dollers' used for soldiers' pay; and in October 1642 the Earl of Newcastle is recorded as having received, at Newcastle, a barrel of 'ducatoons', amounting to £500 sterling, in one of the Queen's arms shipments from Holland. With no mint at that stage to recoin them, he no doubt distributed them as such (ducatons have turned up in several Yorkshire hoards). Henrietta Maria herself arrived in Yorkshire at the end of February 1642/3, with large quantities of supplies, including coin, if the rumours which reached the Venetian ambassador in London are to be believed. The advent of troops from Scotland and Ireland, both countries where European coins played a significant rôle, may also have brought foreign specie to England. Prize goods are another source, such as the five barrels of dollars, bound for merchants in Exeter, which were included amongst goods seized by Parliament's Lord Admiral, the Earl of Warwick, in June 1644.

A proclamation which was issued by the royalist administration in Oxford on 4 March 1643/4 made a number of foreign coin types legal

BY THE KING.

¶ *A Proclamation for making of severall pieces of Forreigne Coyne to be Currant in this Kingdome, for the furtherance of the Trade thereof.*

HEREAS, upon deliberate and mature debate and consideration had with Our Privy-Councell, and consideration had of the opinions, as well of the Masters and Wardens of Our Mint, as of severall Merchants and others of good experience and understanding in Trade, It is conceived, that it would conduce much to the advancement and quickning of Trade in these distracted times, and the taking off the Cloth and Manufactures of this Kingdome, if the severall pieces or species of Forreigne Coyne hereafter specified, were made currant within this our Kingdom of England, and dominion of Wales, at the rates and values herein also mentioned; We have ~~......~~ with advice of Our Privy-Councell publish this Our Proclamation, and doe hereby ordaine, appoynt, and Declare, That from and after the date of this Our Proclamation, and untill We shall otherwise ordaine, and that Our pleasure shall be Published and Declared to the Contrary, these Peices or species of Forreign Coyn, that is to say the *Ducatoone* weighing one ounce and twenty graines; The Imperiall *Rix Dollers* weighing Eighteen penny weight and twelve graines; The *Crosse Dollers*, weighing Eighteen penny weight; The Spanish peices of *Eight* weighing Seventeen penny weight and twelve graines; The *Quartdecue* of France weighing Six penny weight and fower graines; The *Double Ryder* of the Low Countries, weighing equall with the two and twenty shillings peice of the Coyne of Our deare Father King JAMES of Blessed memory; And the Spanish *Double Pistoll* weighing fower penny weight and eight graines, shall be currant mony within this our Kingdom of England and Dominion Wales, and shall be so accompted; and shall be taken accepted and allowed in all Payments and Receipts, at and for the respective rates and values hereafter specified, that is to say, the *Ducatoone* weighing as aforesaid, at and for the rate or value of Five shillings & sixpence currant mony of England; The Imperiall *Rix Doller* weighing as aforesaid, at and for the rate or value of Fower shillings and eight pence; The *Crosse Doller* weighing as aforesaid, at and for the rate or value of Fower shillings and six pence; The Spanish peices of *Eight*, weighing as aforesaid, at and for the rate or value of Fower shillings and six pence; The *Quartdecue* of France weighing as aforesaid, at and for the rate or value of one shilling and sixpence; The *Double Rider* of the Low Countries weighing as aforesaid, at and for the rate and value of one Pound one Shilling and sixpence; And the Spanish *Double Pistoll* weighing as aforesaid, at and for the rate or value of Fifteen shillings of currant mony of England. And We doe hereby Require and Command all Persons whatsoever within this Our Kingdom of England and Dominion of Wales, to accept and allow of the said Pieces of Forreign Coyne of the severall and respective weights before mentioned, at and for the severall rates and values aforesaid, in all payments and Receipts. *Given at Our Court at* Oxford, *the fourth day of March,* 1643.

GOD SAVE THE KING.

¶ *Printed at* Oxford, *by* Leonard Lichfield, *Printer to the University,* 1643.

Fig. 100 Charles I, proclamation regarding the currency of foreign coin; Oxford, 4 March 1643/4. *British Library.*

tender at rates very close to their intrinsic values (**100** and Table IV), ostensibly for the 'advancement and quickning of trade in these distracted times' and probably in tacit recognition of their existing place in the currency.

Table IV: *Proclaimed and intrinsic values of foreign coin*

	Oxford Proclamation March 1643/4	Tower Mint assays, January 1650/1 (value as coins)
SILVER		
Ducatoon	5s 6d	5s 6⅛d
Rix Doller	4s 8d	4s 7¾d
Crosse Doller	4s 6d	4s 4¾d
Piece of Eight	4s 6d	4s 6½d
Cardecue	1s 6d	1s 7d
GOLD		
Double Ryder	£1 1s 6d	£1 1s 11½d
Double Pistoll	£0 15s 0d	£0 14s 8⅔d

Of the gold types in the Oxford proclamation, a half-rijder (*cf.* **101**) was included in a hoard found at Newark and Spanish double escudos ('double pistolls', *cf.* **102**) have been found in Lincolnshire and Glamorgan. Of the silver types, there are few records of finds of Spanish or Spanish-American eight-real pieces and none (in a Civil War context) of the cardecues or German Reichstaler ('Rix Dollers'), but ducatons (**103**) and patagons ('Crosse Dollers', **104**) of the Spanish Netherlands are by far the most commonly found, notably in the two recent hoards from Breckenbrough, North Yorkshire and Caunton, Nottinghamshire.

Fig. 101 United Netherlands, Province of Utrecht, gold grote gouden rijder, 1617. Current in England and Wales at £1 1s 6d.

Fig. 102 Spain, Philip IV (1621–65), gold 2-escudos, Seville 1623 (or perhaps 21). Current for 15s. These crudely-made 'cobs' rarely display more than a portion of their designs.

Fig. 103 Spanish Netherlands, Philip IV (1621–65), silver ducaton, Antwerp (mint-signature, a hand), 1634. Current for 5s 6d.

Fig. 104 Spanish Netherlands, Albert and Isabella (1598–1621), silver patagon, Antwerp 1619. Current for 4s 6d.

Chapter 8

Siege Coinages of the Civil War

Towards the end of the war, many towns and castles in royalist hands had become isolated. In the artificial conditions within a besieged stronghold, there was often no need for money. At Lathom House, Lancashire, for instance, the soldiers shared out their cash by the handful to use as stakes for span-counter (shove-halfpenny), which they played to while away their time. During the siege of York there was an efficient system of free billeting, charged to the officers and gentry. In a few cases, however, 'money of necessity' was coined in an attempt to pay the garrison and to maintain day-to-day transactions. It was no novelty: the idea of siege money will have been familiar to those who had served in the European wars of the preceding decades. Such issues were produced by local governors acting on their own authority and are characterized by simple designs and often by unusual shapes and weight standards. During 1645–6 three garrisons issued their own coins and all of these issues are attested by some form of contemporary reference.

Carlisle mint

In the wake of Marston Moor, Carlisle became an isolated royalist outpost in the far north, and from October 1644 the city was besieged (or rather blockaded) by a Scots army under David Leslie, who was content to wait until shortage of provisions and despair of relief forced a negotiated surrender. Its governor was Sir Thomas Glemham, previously at York, and the man to whom would also fall the dubious honour of surrendering the King's capital, Oxford.

Isaac Tullie, a 17-year-old resident of the town, described the course of the siege in considerable detail. It was a leisurely affair. 'The daily skirmishes were none of them for the defence of the walls, which the enemy never assaulted, but about the fetching in of cattle . . . and now and then the slighting of a work. More was the pity, that such brave men as the besieged should be confined to such worthless adventures as these . . .'. There were lighter moments: on 28 March 1645, 'the pleasantness of the day invited Sr Thomas Glemham, with many other Gent. and Gentlewomen, to take the air near Bocherby; against whom the enemy drawing out all their horse, stood to see them course a haire and take it, under their noses'.

Tullie also noted that towards the end 'an order was published to every citizen to bring in their plate to be coyned, which they did chearfully', though they were not thereby exempted from sudden searches for money or plate on their premises. On 30 May 1645 'three shillings pieces were coined out of the cyttysens plate'. A note dated 13 May 1645 gives details of 1,162 oz taken from the city and from 41 citizens, Tullie's mother's contribution being five spoons weighing 6¼ oz. Of this, after loss in melting and working, 1,076 oz were coined at six shillings per ounce into £323, a gain of over £54 of coined specie when set against the normal value of five shillings. Two denominations, shillings and three-shillings, were produced with similar designs (**105, 115**).

The news of Naseby finally killed all hope of relief, and the city all but ran out of food. The last barrel of strong ale, however, was put to good use. On 23 June, a Scots commander came into the city to negotiate its surrender, but returned to Leslie so drunk that he could give him 'no account of his errand, nor utter a wise word'. Next day a 'graver person' was sent in, but fared no better, returning in 'the same pickle . . ., professing that the garrison was everywhere full of strong drink'. The city surrendered the following day.

Fig. 105 Carlisle besieged, shilling, May 1645. The letters OBS are short for the Latin *obsessum*, 'besieged', or perhaps *obsidio*, 'siege' (cf. also **109**).

Scarborough mint

Scarborough was held for the King by Sir Hugh Chomley, previously a parliamentarian. After Marston Moor and the loss of York, he obtained a 20-day truce in which to negotiate the town's surrender, sending 19 propositions to the Committee of Both Kingdoms in London whose reply, dated 26 August 1644, rejected several. Chomley had used the truce to fortify the town and to gather the harvest and other provisions, so he was well prepared for a protracted siege.

By February 1644/5 Chomley was forced to abandon the town, and Sir John Meldrum made strenuous efforts, which eventually cost him his life, to storm the castle. The garrison held out, in increasingly desperate straits until surrendering on terms on 22 July. Chomley tried personally to pay his garrison not only for their upkeep but also sixpence per man per day for their labour in repairing the daily breaches in the walls. His memoir of the siege describes the genesis of siege money:

> 'att last when he wanted money, and could not borrowe, having likewise solde the small quantities of plaite hee had there to defray the publicke chardge, hee made a motion that everie one that had anie plaite in the garrison might contribute some part of it to the reliefe of the soldiers, but those whoe had more than double to what was in the garrison besides, were not onlie unwilling to part with any themselves, but underhand wrought upon others to be adverse to itt; so that rather than to breed the least disquiett by taking any man's goods against his will, the Governor made use of the plaite which belonged to some persons hee had particuler interest in, which was cutt in pieces, and passed currant according to there several weights, some of them had the stampe of a broaken castle with this inscription, 'Caroli fortuna resurgam'; by this meanes the officers and soldiers, which began to be very clamorous, were for the present verie well settled . . .'.

Two series of silver 'coins' have been attributed to Scarborough with a range of over 20 different denominations from 5s 8d down to fourpence confirming Sir Hugh's comment on their values (**106, 107**). All are very rare and the series is bedevilled by later forgeries. On one series we may see clearly the 'broaken castle' (**106**), but no genuine specimen bears the legend 'Caroli fortuna resurgam'. Such objects exist, but are now thought to be eighteenth-century concoctions (**108**).

Fig. 106 Scarborough besieged, shilling, (1645), bearing the 'stampe of a broaken castle'. *British Museum.*

Fig. 107 Scarborough besieged, one shilling and four-pence. This second type, which dovetails neatly into the range of values of Scarborough siege coins, was at one time attributed to Beeston Castle. *British Museum.*

Fig. 108 *'Caroli Fortuna Resurgam'* ('I, fortune of Charles, shall rise again'): variously attributed to Scarborough and Colchester in the past, it now seems likely that none of these pieces is a contemporary siege issue. They may have been made as souvenirs (note the lack of a mark of value), or in the eighteenth century for collectors. *British Museum.*

Newark mint

Newark, which controlled an important centre of communications on the river Trent in the East Midlands, was a royalist fortress from about Christmas 1642, when the Earl of Newcastle placed a garrison there, until the end of the war in England. It enabled them to keep open a supply route between Oxford and Yorkshire while they still held the north, and posed a strategic threat to the parliamentarian heartlands of eastern England as well as acting as a base for local raiding. Three attempts were made to take the town: an attempted storming in February 1642/3; the siege from 29 February to 21 March 1643/4, the relief of which by Prince Rupert resulted in the capture of Meldrum's entire besieging army; and the final siege from November 1645 to 8 May 1646, when the garrison surrendered by order of the King, who had just given himself up to the Scots army at Southwell, not far away.

Coins were produced in Newark during this final siege. They are of a single basic design, struck on lozenge-shaped blanks in four denominations (halfcrown, shilling, ninepence and sixpence), dated 1645 and 1646 (**109, 115**). Their engraving is competent and the weights correspond with contemporary official coinage standards. Many of the smaller coins were made directly from cut-up plate, including a series dated 1646 produced from gilt plate. Some of these have reeded edges and marks where areas of gilding have worn off through use before coining; others bear a royal coat of arms, even the occasional hallmark, overstruck by the Newark designs. A royal service of gilt plate of early Stuart date seems to have been sacrificed during the final weeks of the siege.

There are two contemporary references to the Newark siege coinage, both pictorial. A 1645 ninepence is depicted on a plan of the siege (**110**), surveyed by Richard Clampe, a parliamentarian engineer who was an eyewitness and perhaps even responsible for laying out the besiegers' lines as well as recording them. The plan was engraved by Peregrine Lovell (for whom no work later than 1647 is known) and printed and sold by Peter Stent of London, almost certainly before 1650.

The coins themselves have survived in considerable numbers and seem to have been prized as souvenirs – many have been pierced for suspension or attachment to clothing. When Anthony Ascham, Commonwealth ambassador to Spain, was murdered in Madrid in June 1650, a Newark shilling, perhaps retooled as an amulet if the drawing that was published is to be believed, was found on his body 'on his left side next his skinne'. Their currency, however, was strictly local and the only modern find of siege money of any sort consisted of two 1646 Newark ninepences found with other coins accompanying a skeleton buried on the outskirts of Newark itself.

Fig. 109 'Newarke' besieged, shilling, 1645. One of the first coins of the siege: many of 1645 and all dated 1646 use the more familiar 'Newark' (cf. **115**).

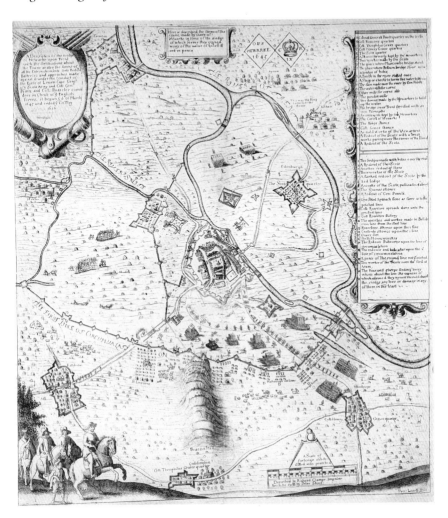

Fig. 110 Richard Clampe's plan of the siege of Newark, 1646, showing royalist and parliamentarian fortifications and a Newark siege coin. (size of original 20 × 17 inches, 509 × 432 mm). *British Library.*

The Second Civil War: Colchester and Pontefract

The royalist risings of 1648, collectively termed the 'Second Civil War', were quickly crushed. In South Wales, an army led by Major General Rowland Laugharne (as a Parliament man the successful besieger of Aberystwyth Castle in 1646) was defeated at St Fagans, near Cardiff on 8 May. An army formed in Kent was driven into Essex and retreated to Colchester, which fell to Fairfax only after a bitter siege lasting from 13 June to 28 August. Coins are said to have been produced by the defenders, notably a gold ten-shilling piece in the British Museum (**111**), which may be a relic of the siege (though there is no contemporary corroboration) and '*Caroli fortuna resurgam*' pieces which certainly are not. Eventually, shortage of food and ammunition forced the garrison to surrender. The royalist commanders rendered themselves 'to mercy', which for Sir George Lisle and Sir Charles Lucas meant summary execution.

Fig. 111 Gold 'ten shilling piece' dated 1648. This is possibly a relic of the Colchester siege, but does not seem to belong to an 'official' issue. *British Museum.*

The Yorkshire castle of Pontefract, the 'key to the north' (**112**), was seized for the King in a bloodless coup by Colonel John Morris on 2 June 1648, but the defeat of the invading Scots army by Cromwell at Preston (17 August) left it isolated and from October the castle underwent its third siege of the war years. The siege was at first desultory, but the arrival of General Rainsborough and his subsequent killing at Doncaster in a daring royalist commando raid led to a more vigorous and close siege by General Lambert. Even so, the garrison held out until 22 March 1648/9, nearly two months after Charles I's death. Their leaders, as at Colchester, were excepted from mercy, but most contrived to escape. Morris and a companion were eventually captured and executed. By 5 April 1649, the castle had been demolished, at a cost of £1,779 17s 4d, which was all recouped by selling the materials, notably lead, which alone raised over £1,500.

Two series of coins, mainly shillings but including gold twenty-shillings, were struck by the defenders, before (**113**) and after the

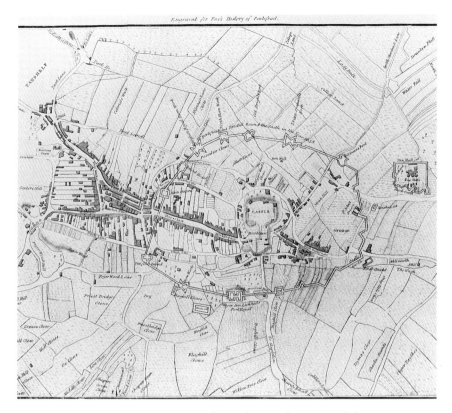

Fig. 112 Plan of Pontefract, showing locations of the siege works of 1648, from G. Fox, *The History of Pontefract*, 1827.

Fig. 113 Pontefract besieged, lozenge-shaped shilling, 1648. Note the flaw on the C of P-C, which thus resembles P-O, and the possible remains of a date letter or other hallmark at the top of the obverse.

Fig. 115 'Siege Coins': an engraving from *Coins, Medals, Ancient Buildings and other Antiquities relative to the English History*, published by R. Bowyer, 1794. The coins, which are faithfully depicted, are: a. Newark halfcrown 1646; b. '*Caroli Fortuna Resurgam*', probably eighteenth-century (cf. **108**); c. Pontefract shilling, struck before the King's death; d. Pontefract shilling of Charles II (cf. **113**); e. Carlisle three shillings, 1645; f. Scarborough halfcrown (?), with later engraving on reverse. The engraver, John Landseer, was the father of the celebrated Victorian Academician, Sir Edwin. *British Museum.*

King's death, the second series being the first coins to be struck in the name of Charles II (**114** and **Colour Plate IX**). A Pontefract coin (perhaps of the type of **113**) is mentioned in a contemporary newspaper, *The Kingdom's Faithful and Impartial Scout*:

> [Monday, February 5th] ... The besieged have lately made two sallies forth but repulsed without any great losse to us; in the last ... we took two of theirs prisoners, one of which had a small parcel of silver in his pocket, somewhat square; on the one side thereof was stamped a castle with PO [*recte*, P-C] for Pontefract, and on the other was a crown with CR on each side of it. These pieces they make of plate, which they get out of the country, and pass among them for coyn.

Fig. 114 Pontefract besieged, shilling dated 1648 in the name of Charles II: 'for the son, after the father's death'.

Chapter 9

Ireland

Events in Ireland also left their mark on the contemporary coinage. The revolt of October 1641 led to the establishment of an insurgent Catholic government in Kilkenny, while English control was restricted to the area around Dublin and an enclave in Munster centred on present day County Cork. The need to suppress the rebellion brought to a head the tensions between King and Parliament over control of the armed forces in the months leading to civil war in England itself.

Both sides in the Irish conflict minted 'coinages of necessity'. The Confederated Catholics in Kilkenny produced copper small change and two issues of silver. The first was ordered on 15 November 1642 to be coined from plate with the 'ordinary stamp used in the moneyes now currant', and has been identified with the crude halfcrowns known as Blacksmith's Money (**116**). These copy Tower halfcrowns from the early part of the reign, i.e. 'money now currant' in that since 1637 payments in English money had been obligatory in Ireland, replacing the various 'Irish' and foreign types which had hitherto circulated. A second explanation of the type also ascribes it to Kilkenny, as an issue of the royalists in 1649 (see below). The second silver issue, known as 'Rebel Money' was produced during 1643 and consisted of crowns and halfcrowns bearing as designs a large cross and their respective values (**117**).

The Lords, Justices and Council of Ireland appealed repeatedly for both troops and money from England to suppress the rebellion. In

Fig. 116 Halfcrown, 'Blacksmiths Money', p.m.'s *Cross* and *Harp*. Probably struck at Kilkenny by the Confederate Catholics in 1642. Were it Ormonde's Kilkenny issue of 1649, the title 'CAROLVS.II.' might be expected. *British Museum.*

Fig. 117 'Rebel Money', silver crown of reduced weight (24.43 g), traditionally ascribed to the Confederate Catholics. It has also been suggested that this coinage may have been issued by officials at Dublin Castle under Col. Michael Jones, Deputy Governor under the English Parliament, *c.* 1648.

Fig. 118 Halfcrown of the Lords Justices first issue, 1642/3. The design is the same on both sides and the declared weight (9 dwt and 16 grains, or 15.03 grammes) matches that of an English halfcrown.

Fig. 119 'Annulets' groat of the Lords Justices first issue. *British Museum.*

January 1642/3 they collected plate in Dublin (about £1,200 worth) which was turned into silver coinage stamped with the weights of each denomination (**118**); on some of the smallest (9d, 6d, 4d and 3d) the value in pence was also indicated by a number of small rings, the so-called 'Annulets issue' (**119**). A second group of crowns and half-crowns was simply stamped with the appropriate value ('Dublin Money'). These coins were all produced to Tower standards of weight and fineness.

Fig. 121 William Butler, 12th Earl (afterwards 1st Duke)
of Ormonde; attributed to Justus van Egmont (1601–74).
Claydon House; photograph by Peter Clayton.

A further coinage, for which royal approval was sought and received, was proclaimed in Dublin on 8 July 1643. Its designs were specified by the King in a letter written from Oxford on 25 May, and the standards again matched the English. The Lords Justices were authorized to melt down plate, etc., into

> small peeces, to the value of five shillings, halfe-crowns, twelve-pences, six-pences, or of any less value, which several small peeces they shall make the same waight, value and allay, as our moneys now currant in England of those value respectively are, and shall stamp the same on the one side, with these letters (scilicet) C.R. for Carolus Rex, with a crown over those letters, and on the other side with the values of the said severall peeces respectively.

Fig. 120 Shilling of the Lords Justices issue of 1643–4, called 'Ormonde Money'.

The new coinage (**120**) was produced by Sir John Veale and two prominent Dublin goldsmiths, Peter Vandenhoven and Gilbert Tonques, who entered into a recognizance of £2,000 for the true making of the coins, which were to be delivered to the bringers of the plate – in the normal fashion, that is. An eighth part was required to be coined as groats, threepences and twopences. On 13 October 1643, the issue was declared legal tender in England, no doubt with an eye to the forces recently freed by the truce ('cessation') of 15 September to leave for England to fight for the King. There are, however, no confirmed instances of these coins being found in England or Wales. This coinage is commonly known as 'Ormonde money' – James Butler, 12th Earl and subsequently 1st Duke of Ormonde, Lieutenant-General of the King's forces in Ireland and later Lord-Lieutenant, was a signatory of the July proclamation (**121**).

Ormonde was responsible for two further issues of coinage in Ireland. On 29 July 1646 he authorized Vandenhoven and Tonques to produce gold 'pledges' from bullion to hand, to be marked with their weights (4 pennyweight 7 grains and 8 dwt 14 gr), equivalent to Spanish pistoles and double pistoles current in Ireland, though at a lower fineness of 19 carats (79%). On 1 February 1646/7 civilians were encouraged to submit bullion for similar coining, but at a higher fineness ('betwixt 20 and 22 carrotts': 83.3 − 91.6%), corresponding to that of the Spanish coins. Ormonde's gold (122) is extremely rare today − only two double pistoles, which survived in the collection of the Earls of Bridgewater, and eleven pistoles are known, six of these from a single hoard found in 1946−8 at Derryville, Portarlington, Co. Laois.

Fig. 122 Gold double pistole of Ormonde's 1646 or 1646/7 issue. *British Museum.*

In July 1647 Ormonde left Ireland, having handed Dublin over to a parliamentary expedition. However, he returned in September 1648 to lead a united royalist alliance, and silver crowns and halfcrowns similar to those of the second 1643 issue, bearing the name and titles of Charles II, were probably issued by him in 1649 (123); their place of minting is uncertain (it cannot be Dublin). It is tempting to associate this issue with Ormonde's warrant of 8 August 1649 for establishing a mint at Kilkenny (which remained in royalist hands until 28 March 1650), but this specified 'the coyning of gould and silver according to the way manner and form formerly used in England . . .' which might in some ways accord better with the 'Blacksmith' halfcrowns, though it is uncertain whether Ormonde's Kilkenny mint ever functioned. Some crude copper 'coins' from Bandon, Cork, Kinsale and Youghal (the last dated 1646), long held to be siege or necessity issues of the southern 'cities of refuge', are now regarded as an early and crude

Fig. 123 Halfcrown in the name of Charles II, issued by Ormonde in 1649.

Fig. 124 Token farthing for the English enclave in Munster, Youghal 1646. *British Museum.*

segment of the Irish token series. The Youghal pieces (**124**) were proclaimed at Cork on 20 March 1645/6, to be current throughout the English enclave as small change, with provisions for their exchange and limits on the amounts qualifying as legal tender, reminiscent of the farthing tokens in England. Silver shillings and sixpences were, however, struck in Cork in 1647.

Fig. 125 Tower halfcrown, privy-mark *Triangle-in-circle*, 1641−3; from the Penybryn hoard.

Fig. 126 Tower gold twenty shillings, p.m. *P-in-brackets*, under parliamentary control, 1643−4.

Figs. 127−8 Tower halfcrown and shilling, both with p.m. *R-in-brackets*, under Parliament, 1644−5. Despite appearances, both are unworn coins of full weight, but poorly produced. The shilling comes from the Penybryn hoard.

Chapter 10

The Tower Mint in the Civil War

Parliament seized control of the Mint in the Tower on 10 August 1642, though it was not until 5 October that the staff were formally forbidden to leave their posts. The joint masters, Sir Ralph Freeman and Sir Thomas Aylesbury were ejected; the Warden, Sir William Parkhurst had joined the King, and was to become Charles's joint master at the Oxford mint (**52**). Aylesbury, too, reappeared at Oxford, though not in the context of the mint (p. 35). In the event, few others had joined the King: most mint workers took the simplest course and remained where they were. (In the same way, those moneyers seconded to Bushell at Aberystwyth served the royalists at Shrewsbury, Oxford and Bristol.) There was plenty of work at the Tower: to the continuing massive amounts of Spanish silver were added large quantities of plate contributed more or less voluntarily by the citizens of London and those of Puritan persuasion elsewhere.

The Parliament, anxious to maintain the fiction that it was fighting on behalf of the King, was reluctant to usurp the royal prerogative of coining, especially since at first military success was by no means certain. The appearance of the coins thus remained the same and their dies continued to be made from the same design- and letter-punches. The annual alteration of the privy-mark and pyx trial were overlooked in the spring of 1642, though an interim account of bullion melted and coined in the period 1 April 1641 to 31 March 1642 was drawn up. The existing mark, a triangle within a circle, continued in use for a further year. The coins bearing this mark therefore tend to dominate the Civil War hoards, not only because so many were struck (about £2 million in silver alone), but also because it was the last Tower issue to pass into circulation throughout the country before communications became difficult (**125**). A new master was not appointed until 6 May 1643, when Sir Robert Harley returned to the post he had previously held from 1626 until 1635. At the same time, a new privy-mark, 'P-in-brackets' (**126**), hinted that control of the Mint now lay with Parliament, and the 'triangle-in-circle' coins were finally pyxed.

Output continued at a high level during the war years (about £1 million each year, 95% of it in silver) fuelled mainly by the Spanish silver. Weight and fineness were maintained, but many coins were poorly produced. The Mint had taken delivery of five iron presses of unspecified type in 1640 and a further eleven in 1641/2, but it was not a good time for experiment. There is no hint from the products that

Table V: *The Tower Mint: Privy-marks and pyx trials under Parliament,*
1643−9

⊕	Triangle-in-circle	29 May 1643
(P)	P-in-brackets	15 July 1644
(R)	R-in-brackets	12 May 1645
👁	Eye	10 November 1645
☼	Sun	15 February 1646/7
✝	Sceptre	9 November 1649

these were ever used: the coins show every sign of having been made by traditional manual methods, at great speed (**127−8**).

The areas controlled by Parliament always formed a more coherent whole than those of the royalists. Lines of communication were better established, with control of the capital, all routes leading from it and most of the south and east coasts. No branch mints were opened, although the *Commons Journal* for 8 December 1642 records that the Committee for the Safety of the Tower were ordered to confer and consult with the officers and moneyers of the Mint, concerning the 'translating or erecting of a mint in the city of *Exon*', presumably to take advantage of Parliament's control of the prosperous county of Devon. On 3 January 1642/3 this was referred to the Committee of Dispatches, to provide a mint and moneyers and to send them down to Exeter. Nothing further is heard of such a mint, though if it had used Tower Mint dies its products would be very hard to identify. In September 1643, after a siege lasting two and a half months, Exeter fell to the royalists, who promptly established their own mint there, as we have seen.

Nevertheless, the increasing scale of the war effort brought problems of cash flow for Parliament, just as for the royalists. On 22 July 1643 an ordinance was passed for the 'Speedy Raising and Levying of Monies, set by way of a charge or new Impost, on ... commodities', such as tobacco, wine, beer and various imported groceries and goods, otherwise known as the Excise. It was promptly imitated by the royalists and despite both sides' protestations that it would be 'laide down and utterly abolished' at the end of the war it remains with us today. In 1644, Parliament found it necessary to limit immediate costs by paying only a proportion of the sums owing in soldiers' pay, and issuing certificates promising repayment, or personal debentures.

The case of the army of the Eastern Association gives us some idea of the costs involved. Its monthly pay, based on a muster in September 1644, has been estimated at around £31,000, though in the event the cavalry each received only 126 days' pay in 1644 and the infantry around 250 (and this army was better paid than some). Similarly, a subsidy of £30,000 per month was promised as the price of the Scots entering England on Parliament's side, but special efforts to raise this sum (**129**) failed to ensure that they were paid in full when they finally arrived in 1644, and the inhabitants of northern England suffered accordingly. It is little wonder that the smaller, distant, but important armies of the Fairfaxes in Yorkshire and Sir William Brereton in Cheshire were forever waiting for their pay. On 18 June 1644 Ferdinando

Y Vertue of an ordinance of *Both* Houfes, of the 27 of *October*, 1643, whereby
is to bee levyed by way of Loane in the County of   for
the better inabling of our Brethren the *Scots*, for our affiftance, we doe in purfuance thereof, and according to the powers derived unto us, Affeffe you to lend the fumme of
to be paid within eight
dayes unto   at
whofe Acquittance for the fame being fubfigned and entered as is directed, fhall be fufficient for you to receive the faid fumme, with the Vfe for the forbearance thereof, at the rate of eight pound *per centum, per annum,* according to the true intent of the faid Ordinance.

Fig. 129 Parliamentary assessment for the levy to pay the Scots army, October 1643. Another forced loan, bearing notional interest at the standard 8%. *British Library.*

Lord Fairfax (father of Sir Thomas), who estimated that his army pay came to £15,000 per month, wrote to London from his quarters outside York that he had only received £10,000 in the past four months.

Meanwhile, what was happening to the continuing massive output of silver from the Mint? It is clear that large amounts of money were withdrawn from circulation by hoarding at this time. The new money seems to have been used in the south-east, for instance in purchasing supplies, and then to have gone to ground in the parliamentarian heartlands, exemplified by a large hoard found at Ashdon, Essex, in 1984, which contained considerable numbers of mint-fresh Tower coins struck in the years 1643–5.

Like their royalist counterparts, the parliamentarians produced medals to commemorate events and personalities and as military rewards. The Earl of Essex, Sir William Waller, the Earl of Manchester, Ferdinando Lord Fairfax and his son Sir Thomas (**130**) were among commanders depicted, for the most part, on oval badges. Several are the work of Thomas Simon, who with Edward Wade was appointed joint chief engraver on 4 April 1645, following the death of Edward Green (chief engraver, 1626–45). Simon, whose work was to dominate the coins and medals of the Commonwealth and Protectorate, was apprenticed to Green on 25 September 1635 and also learned much from the work of Briot. The 'Scots Rebellion' medals of 1639 are early works of his (**70**). By the time his apprenticeship ended, war was breaking out. He remained loyal to Parliament and in 1643 committed what the royalists regarded as high treason by engraving a duplicate Great Seal for Parliament's use after the original had been taken to the King at York.

Fig. 130 Sir Thomas Fairfax, gold military reward by Thomas Simon, 1645; probably awarded to officers who had served under Fairfax at Marston Moor. Perhaps the greatest of Parliament's generals, Fairfax was also scrupulously fair to defeated royalists (notably, in our context, Sir Richard Vyvyan). When Oxford surrendered Fairfax's first act was to 'sett a good guard of soldiers to preserve the Bodleian Library' (Aubrey). On occasion, he could be ruthless, as in the execution of Lucas and Lisle at Colchester in 1648. *British Museum.*

Fig. 131 Tower crown, p.m. *Sun*, 1645–46/7, with new equestrian portrait attributed to Thomas Simon. *British Museum.*

Fig. 132 Tower shilling, p.m. *Sceptre*, 1646/7–48/9.

In spite of his surrender in 1646 and subsequent captivity, Charles remained King and the coinage continued to be struck in his name. New portrait punches were prepared and although there may be an element of caricature in some of these, the equestrian effigy which was introduced in 1646 is a fine creation, coming closest of all to a naturalistic and realistically-scaled depiction (**131**). It is normally attributed to Thomas Simon and is very similar to his design approved for halfcrowns of Charles II's first coinage in 1660, which was not in the event used. Output from the Tower dropped dramatically in 1647 as the Thirty Years War drew towards its end and the Spanish found it cheaper to use Dutch carriers to transport their silver. The coins of Charles's last years are therefore relatively rare, but much improved in appearance, as the moneyers were once again able to give enough care to their work (**132**).

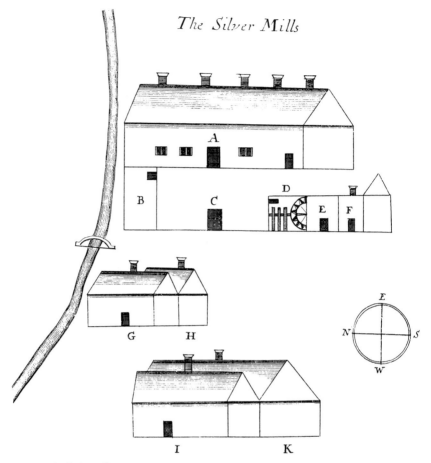

The Silver Mills

A *The Silver Mills with five furnices*
B *The Old Mint House*
C *The Yard*
D *The Stamping Mill*
E *The Mill to Grind the Bone ashes*
F *The Smiths forge*
G *The old Refining house*
H *The Reduceing house*
I *The old Red-lead Mills*
K *The house wher' we now mould y.e Starbright Brick*

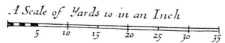

A Scale of Yards 10 in an Inch

Fig. 133 The Silver Mills, Talybont, Cardiganshire, showing the Old Mint House (at B). From W. Waller, *An Account of the Cardiganshire Mines*, 1699.

Aberystwyth revived

With conditions relatively settled and with new silver once again scarce, the revival of the Welsh branch mint became an attractive proposition. On 6 March 1646/7 Edmund Goodere, Bushell's partner in the Cardiganshire mines, petitioned the House of Lords for permission to reopen the Aberystwyth mint, but at 'a place called the smelting mills, near the refining house', on account of the siege-damage to the castle at Aberystwyth, where the pre-war mint had been situated (p. 15). The premises, between Talybont and Machynlleth, subsequently became the iron-smelting Dyfi Furnace, where recent excavations have shown that few traces now remain of the seventeenth-century 'silver mills' phase (**133**). As before, the Tower Mint provided dies and workmen. The date of the re-opening is not known, but the small output may have been made late in 1648. The King's execution on 30 January 1648/9 was soon followed by closure of the mint, and its dies and equipment were surrendered to a parliamentary representative on 23 February.

The coins struck at the Silver Mills are similar in design to prewar Aberystwyth products, but with a crown as privy-mark (**134–7**). The

Figs. 134–7 Halfcrown, sixpence, threepence and half-groat struck at the Silver Mills, 1648–48/9, all with p.m. *Crown* and the Welsh feathers.

same denominations were made, excepting only halfpence. These types were for a long time assigned to a mythical mint at Combe Martin in Devon, whose flooded silver mines Bushell attempted to revive in 1648, but the 'Welsh' design and the close correspondence of surviving coins to the list of dies surrendered at the Silver Mills suggest that the 'crown' coins are indeed the products of the briefly-restored Aberystwyth operation. Confirmation comes from the isotopic analysis of lead traces, which indicates that these coins are made of silver from the same source as that used for prewar Aberystwyth issues.

Chapter 11

Aftermath

The story of the Civil War and its coinage does not end with the death of Charles I. As we have seen the siege of Pontefract was maintained, and military action in Scotland and Ireland continued until 1652. Britain was to remain a republic for a further eight years before Charles II returned in 1660, in what he termed the twelfth year of his reign. This last chapter therefore describes some of the coins and medals of the final phase of the Great Rebellion and its aftermath.

Commonwealth and Protectorate, 1649–60

The Kingly office was abolished by Act of Parliament on 17 March 1648/9 and Thomas Simon was commissioned to cut a new Great Seal for the 'Commonwealth of England'. Meanwhile, moves were under way to establish a new coinage, the Act for which was finally passed on 17 July. In May, Sir Robert Harley was dismissed as Master for refusing to have anything to do with the new coinage and Dr Aaron Guerdain was appointed in his stead. (A pyx trial of Charles I's last ('*Sceptre*') coinage, at Harley's expense, was ordered on 16 May 1649, but not held until 9 November). In a radical departure from previous practice, the legends of the new money were in English and common designs were chosen for all denominations from the gold twenty shillings down to the silver penny (**138–140**), with a simplified version for the tiny halfpenny. These became a standing joke with royalist sympathizers, who described the conjoined shields of the reverse as 'breeches for the Rump' (a reference to the depleted membership of the Long Parliament) and observed from the legends, 'The Commonwealth of England' and 'God with us', that God and the Commonwealth were on different sides.

In 1650, Cromwell's brutal subjugation of the Irish was interrupted when he had to return to the mainland to lead the campaign against the Scots. Despite his being trapped at Dunbar he routed the Scots on 3 September and on the 7th, the Commons resolved that special thanks be conveyed to the Lord-General, also to the officers and soldiers of the army, 'and that a number of gold and silver medals be distributed amongst them'. Thomas Simon was ordered to Scotland to take Cromwell's likeness for the medal. The sitter expressed his own ideas for its design in a letter to the Committee of the Army, 4 February 1650/1:

Figs. 138–140 Commonwealth of England: gold double crown (10 shillings), 1649; silver halfcrown, 1649; undated halfgroat. All of uniform design, struck at the Tower Mint.

It was not a little wonder to me to see that you should send Mr Symonds so great a journey about a business importinge so little as farr as it relates to me, when as if my poore opinion may not be rejected by you, I have to offer to that wch I thinke the most noble end, to witt the comemoracon of that great mercie att Dunbar, & the grauitie to the Army wch might better be expressed upon the meddall by engraving on the one side the Parliam^t wch I heare was intended & will do singularly well, so on the other side an Army wth this inscription over the head of it, The Lord of hosts, wch was o^r word that Day, wherefore if I may begg it as a favo^r from you I most earnestly beseech you if I may doe it w^thout offence that it may be soe, & if you thinke not fitt to have it as I offer, you may alter it as you see Cause only I doe think I may truely say it wilbe verie thankfully acknowledged by me, if you will spare the having my effigies on it.

The Dunbar Medal (**141**) was the first British award intended to be given to officers and men alike for a particular action, but it remains doubtful that a general distribution ever took place, since a recent

Fig. 141 The small 'Dunbar Medal', in gold, by Thomas Simon. Cromwell's request not to appear on the medal was clearly ignored, though an army and the parliamentary watchword were included. *British Museum.*

analysis, by eliminating later restrikes and forgeries, has shown that very few original specimens survive today. The Commonwealth years also saw the beginning of systematic rewarding of meritorious service at sea. The final mainland battle of the Civil War was not fought until 3 September 1651, when Charles II and his Scots army were defeated at Worcester, again by Cromwell.

Attention once again turned to the possibility of mechanizing production of coins and marking their edges, to deter counterfeiting and clipping. Another Frenchman, Pierre Blondeau, was summoned to London, arriving in September 1649; but at first he could not proceed because of opposition from the moneyers. Trials were made in 1651, both by Blondeau and David Ramage, Briot's former pupil, representing the moneyers (**142**). In 1656, Blondeau was ordered to produce a small issue of coins bearing Cromwell's portrait, using dies made by Thomas Simon, newly created chief engraver of the Mint. The project was revived in 1658, but cut short by Cromwell's death, and Blondeau returned to France. The Cromwell coins do not seem to have been issued for circulation, and are not mentioned in the 1661 proclamation which called in the issues of the Commonwealth. Indeed, these regal-looking coins (**143**; compare with **Colour Plate X**, a miniature executed the same year as Simon's portrait) soon commanded a premium as collectors' pieces after the Restoration of Charles II, the diarist Samuel

Fig. 142 Pattern shilling by Blondeau, London 1651. Blondeau's design matches that of the Commonwealth coinage; Ramage varied the designs and omitted the values.

Fig. 143 Oliver Cromwell, halfcrown 1658. The edge of
the coin bears the words HAS:NISI:PERITVRVS:MIHI:
ADIMAT:NEMO (Let no-one remove these from me,
on pain of death), marked by Blondeau's secret new
process.

Pepys noting on 9 March 1661/2 that the silver crowns 'are now sold
it seems for 25s. and 30s. a-piece'. Further examples were made subsequently using new dies cut from Simon's punches, in both London
and the Low Countries.

Provision of the smallest change remained inadequate and the Inter-
regnum saw the beginnings of a rash of token-issues by town corpor-
ations and individual traders, which reached its peak in the first years
of Charles II's reign (see *Further Reading*). Adequate supplies of official
copper farthings and halfpence were eventually produced in the 1670s.

Monarchy restored

On 29 May 1660, Charles II returned to England, and the new King
was showered with petitions for jobs, money, or pardon, from mint-
employees no less than others. Former mint officials loyal to his father
were restored to their positions and an indenture with the newly-
restored Master, Sir Ralph Freeman, provided for coinage of the same
pieces and values as in the time of the late King. Sir William Parkhurst
resumed his post of Warden, jointly with Sir Anthony St Leger.

Thomas Simon sought the post of chief engraver to his Majesty and
the Mint, 'which he had held under the late King, and for pardon,
because by order of Parliament he made their Great Seal in 1643, and
was their Chief Graver of the Mint and seals.' However, Thomas
Rawlins, Charles I's wartime engraver, was restored (at least in name)
on 7 July. Simon seems to have done most of the work and a warrant
dated 25 August 1660 approving designs for the first coins of Charles
II was addressed to him, but he had to be content with the office of
one of the engravers of the King's arms, shields and stamps (31 May
1661). He had not helped his cause by his dilatoriness in producing
the new puncheons and dies, which drew several sharp reminders, and
his former treason in producing a duplicate Great Seal in 1643, for

Parliament's use, had not been forgiven. Rawlins, meanwhile, seems to have worked on seals, such as the judicial seals for the Welsh circuits, completed on 24 September 1660. The new coinage finally appeared in February 1660/1 (**144**). On the 19th, Samuel Pepys saw some of the dies: 'we met with Mr Slingsby [the Deputy Master], ... who showed me the stamps of the King's new coyne; which is strange to see how good they are in the stamp and bad in the money, for lack of skill to make them. But he says Blondeau will shortly come over and then we shall have it better, and the best in the world.' Change was in the air.

Fig. 144 Charles II, Tower shilling, 'first hammered issue', privy-mark *Crown*, *c.* 1660–1. Marks of value were added for the 'second hammered issue'. Continuity and legality are emphasized by the use of the same designs and mottoes as those on his father's coins.

Meanwhile, the coins of the Commonwealth were allowed to circulate for the time being, alongside the 'lawful money'. On 7 September 1661 it was proclaimed that they would cease to be current from the end of November, after which they were to be brought to the Mint and exchanged for an equal quantity of lawful money. (They were, of course, of the same weight and fineness; counterfeiting them continued to carry the same penalties). A period of grace was allowed, during which they continued to be accepted in tax payments. After some discussion, 1 March 1661/2 was made the final deadline for their surrender. The third, and biggest, of Charles II's hammered coinages thus represents the final coinage of the Civil War, as the cross and harp money of the 'late usurpation' went into the melting pot (**Colour Plate XI**). Recoinage seems to have been thorough, even though only some two-thirds of the estimated output of around £1 million was recovered. Much of the rest had no doubt already gone abroad (sold to foreign mints, or servicing a balance of payments deficit) and some was hoarded. Commonwealth coins, notably the smallest types, are occasionally found today in a worn state, while the odd surviving specimen bears the central perforation relating to the great recoinage of 1696. But they are almost never found in post-Restoration hoards, through conscious exclusion as much as scarcity, perhaps.

Fig. 145 The 'Petition Crown' by Thomas Simon, 1663. Fine work, but perhaps too close to life: Roettier's somewhat idealized portraiture was preferred. The legend placed on the edge is a *tour de force* of miniature engraving: **THOMAS SIMON** MOST HVMBLY PRAYS YOVR **MAJESTY** TO COMPARE THIS HIS TRYALL PIECE WITH THE DVTCH AND IF MORE TRVLY DRAWN & EMBOSS'D MORE GRACE FVLLY ORDER'D AND MORE ACCVRATELY ENGRAVEN TO RELEIVE HIM. (Edge enlarged) *British Museum.*

The recoinage was also the last issue to be made at the Tower by traditional methods. In 1661 it was decided to abandon manual techniques in favour of machinery, and on 8 November Simon was sent to France to fetch Blondeau to supervise the mechanization of the Mint, to supply equipment and to train the moneyers in the new methods of coining by mill and press. The famous competition between Thomas Simon and John Roettier, who with his brothers Joseph and Philip was summoned from Flanders by the King, was ordered on 7 February 1661/2. Each artist was to produce a trial piece of crown size for consideration by the King. Roettier's was preferred, perhaps because Simon, the perfectionist, failed to produce his at all. In all events, the famous Petition Crown by Simon is dated 1663, a good year later than the trial itself (**145**).

From February 1662/3 all new money made at the Mint was made mechanically. The long thin ingots were subjected to two rolling operations, after which blanks were made by a screw-driven cutter press. These were then weighed and any which were too heavy were filed and the light were discarded. The blanks were then flattened in batches in a form of vice, blanched, and marked on their edges using Blondeau's machine – such was the fear of counterfeiters, those who operated it were required to swear an oath of secrecy, although such machines were readily to be seen in Paris. Finally they were coined (**146**). Let Samuel Pepys describe the scene:

> The Mill is after this manner; one of the dyes, which hath one side of the piece cut, is fastened to a thing fixed below; and the other dye (they tell me a pair of Dyes will last the marking of 10000 l. before it be worn out, they and all other their tools being made of hardened steel ...) to an engine above, which is moveable by a screw which is pulled by men; and then a piece being clapped by one sitting below between the two dyes, when they meet the impression is set; and then the man with his finger strikes off the piece and claps another on; ... and then another and another, with great speed.
>
> (19 May 1663)

The work was exhausting and for some, hazardous: many moneyers lost one or more finger joints. It was also more expensive than the old way, but speedier and yielded a product that was neater, more consistent, and harder to clip or counterfeit. The coinage had begun to take on the appearance with which we remain familiar today (**147**).

Fig. 146 The screw press in action, from Diderot and D'Alembert's *Encyclopédie*, 1771. This characteristic coining machine of the seventeenth and eighteenth centuries could produce up to 30 coins per minute, and was only superseded when steam powered machines were introduced at the end of the eighteenth century.

Fig. 147 Charles II, Tower shilling, 1671, milled coinage. The reappearance of the Welsh feathers on some of the coins of this year refers to silver sent to the Mint by the company of 'Undertakers for the working of Mines Royal in the counties of Cardigan and Merioneth', which began operations in 1670.

Postscript

What happened to the former royalist mintmasters? All survived and went through a very difficult decade, before the King's return saw them variously compensated for their sacrifices. Sir William Parkhurst, as we have seen, regained his former post of Warden of the Tower Mint, which he held until his death in December 1666. His colleague Thomas Bushell had his right to operate a mint confirmed by Oliver Cromwell and by Richard Cromwell, but it was never again exercised; Bushell pursued various mining projects, but none came to anything. 'The greatest master of the art of running in dept (perhaps) in the world', as John Aubrey described him, had every reason to maintain a low profile, especially when the hoped-for compensation for £36,000 he claimed to have spent on Charles I's behalf failed to materialize. (The loss by fire of account-books, etc. in his former Bristol lodgings on 17 February 1647/8 cannot have helped.) He received only £1,000 of the £3,000 which was finally authorized in 1663. He died in April 1674 in a grace-and-favour garret in Scotland Yard, part of the Palace of Whitehall.

Of the provincial masters, Cary, if we have identified him correctly, may have been the Sir Thomas 'Carey' who petitioned the Committee for Compounding in 1653 after having 'lost many thousands in Ireland by the late rebellion' and may also therefore have been the same Sir Thomas Cary Kt. of Portlester, Co. Meath, whose will was proved in the Prerogative Court of Ireland in 1662.

The Marquess of Newcastle, like many senior royalists, spent the interregnal years in exile, in Antwerp. At the Restoration, he returned to rebuild his shattered estates and to employ his leisure in literature (he wrote poems and plays) and horsemanship, the study and practice of which had led him to publish a major treatise in Antwerp in 1657. He was created Duke of Newcastle on 16 March 1664/5 and died on Christmas Day 1676.

Ormonde served Charles II in exile in France and was rewarded in due course with many honours, including a dukedom. As Lord High Steward of England, he carried the crown at Charles II's coronation. In 1661 he was again made Lord Lieutenant of Ireland, dismissed reluctantly by Charles II in 1669, but reappointed from 1677 to 1685, dying in 1688.

Vyvyan also survived to witness the Restoration. His reward was to be made a gentleman of the Privy Chamber and Captain of St Mawes castle, a Henrician coastal fort which, with Pendennis, guards the approaches to Falmouth and Penryn. The post, which members of his family had held in the past, carried the rank of Captain in the army and a salary of £182 *per annum*. These, and his baronetcy, were his recompense for the royalism that he calculated had cost him almost £10,000. He was MP for St Mawes from 17 March 1662/3 until his death on 3 October 1665 and is buried, with a simple memorial, in the church of St Mawgan-in-Meneage, near Trelowarren.

Royalist issues have necessarily attracted most attention in this survey. Their variety, their links with Charles, King and Martyr, their personal stories and the still unanswered questions associated with them have ensured this pre-eminence ever since they first received scholarly notice during the eighteenth century. The study of hoards and the few surviving output figures suggest, however, that they never accounted for more than a few per cent of the money available at the time, except for the occasional batch fresh from a local mint, as at Pocklington, near York, where new halfcrowns from that mint formed one-third or more of a hoard found in 1849. Indeed, the Earl of Clarendon, royalist historian of the war, described the Shrewsbury mint as 'more for reputation than use'. Past collectors have ensured the disproportionate survival of royalist coins, removed as rarities from the many finds of the eighteenth and nineteenth centuries, whose Tower Mint content then disappeared into the melting pot, its value (as in the 1640s) no more than that of its current silver content. We also owe the survival of the large gold pieces and the smallest silver coins, which were rarely hoarded, to the growth of the coin-collecting habit from the seventeenth century onwards. (Much Commonwealth coinage has no doubt survived for the same reason.)

Nevertheless, as we have seen, the royalist mints played a useful, sometimes vital rôle at local level. Their products, legitimate coins of the realm, continued to circulate down to the great recoinage of 1696, when all available hammered silver money was finally converted into new machine-made coinage. While the Tower Mint provided the bulk of the money handled by soldier and civilian alike, the royalist and other coinages described here give a variety and interest to the currency of England and Wales unmatched at any other time.

Appendix

Sir Richard Vyvyan's Mint Commission, January 3, 1643/4

Charles by the grace of God King of England Scotland ffrance and Ireland defender of the faith **To our trustie** and welbeloved Sir Richard Vivian knight greeting **whereas** our p'sent affaires require the imployment of a mynt within our countyes of Devon and Cornwall and Cittie of Exon, **Knowe yee** that wee reposing speciall trust and confidence in you[r] wisedome skill abilities and care in and for that service doe hereby give you full power and authoritie by your selfe or your sufficient Deputy or Deputyes to erect and sett upp or cause to be erected and sett up one or more mynt or myntes in such place and places within our said Countyes of Devon and Cornewall and Cittie of Exon or in any or either of them as you shall thinke fitt, and to make and engrave or cause to be made and engraven Irons and Stampes with our Effigies Inscriptions and Armes according to our p'sent moneys in our Tower of London, and therewith to instampe and imprint or Cause to be instamped and imprinted all such Ingotts Bullion and plate of Gold or Silver as shalbe from tyme to tyme brought and delivered unto you or unto any such mynt or mynts by any our Subjects. And the moneys soe made and stamped to be of the same species weight and goodnesse as our foresaid moneys in our said Tower of London are and ought to be **and wee** doe further by theis p'sent give full power and authoritie to you the said Sir Richard Vyvyan to doe in manner aforesaid all and every such thing and things in touching and concerning the p'misses, as fully largly and amplie to all intents and purposes as the Officers of our mynt in our said Tower of London lawfully may doe with Ingotts Bullyon or Plate brought to the mynt there to be coyned, **and wee** doe hereby authorize you the said Sir Richard Vyvyan to receive for your paynes and charges in coyning all such Ingotts Bullyon and Plate to be soe brought as aforesaid, the same allowances as in our said Tower are paid, and noe more, without any accompt to be rendered for the same **and our further** will and pleasure is and wee doe hereby will and require you the said Sir Richard Vyvyan to pay or cause to be paid, soe much of the said moneys as shalbe made of all such Ingott Bullyon or Plate as shalbe delivered unto you or your said Deputyes, (or at the said mynt or mynts soe to be erected) by any of our subjects to our use unto our trustie and welbeloved Sir John Berkley Knight or such other p'son or p'sons as wee shall appoint, hee or they giving unto you upon every such payment a Note of Receipt under his or their hand for soe much money as shalbe paid. Which Note or Notes shall be to you a sufficient Discharge against us our heires and Successors in that behalf **and our** will and pleasure is that theis our l'res patent shall have continuance during our pleasure **In witness** whereof we have caused theis our l'res to be made patent **witnes** our selfe att Oxford the third day of January in the Nyneteenth year of our raigne

p b̄re de privato Sigillo

Maps

Map 1. England and Wales during the Civil War, showing locations mentioned in the text.

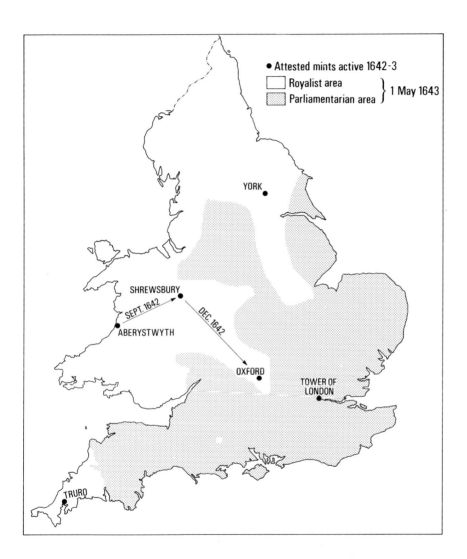

Map 2. The mints of the first campaigns, 1642–3.

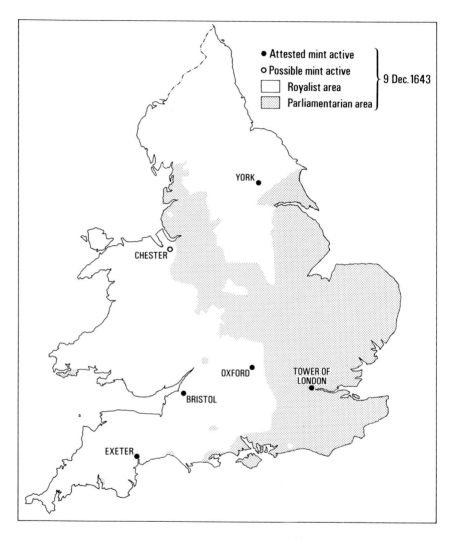

Map 3. Mints in operation at the royalist 'high water
mark'.

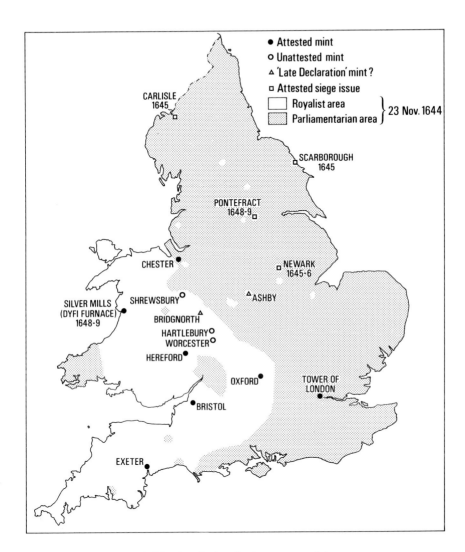

Map 4. Minting during the late stages of the war.

Further Reading

The list that follows can only scratch the surface of the huge literature of the English Civil War, both historical and numismatic — there are many excellent local and regional studies, for instance, whose relevance will vary from reader to reader. The numismatist is well served by the bibliography in North and Preston-Morley (1984).

The Civil War and background

(H BEST) The Account Book of Henry Best, of Elmswell. [1616−44] *Rural Economy in Yorkshire*. Surtees Society **33** 1857:149−64

C E H CHADWICK-HEALY (ed) *Bellum Civile: Hopton's Narrative of his Campaign in the West (1642−1644)*. Somerset Record Soc. **XVIII** 1902

C COOK and J WROUGHTON *English Historical Facts, 1603−1688* London:1980

G DAVIES *The Early Stuarts 1603−1660*. (The Oxford History of England, **IX**) 2nd Ed. Oxford:1959

C DUFFY *Siege Warfare*. London:1979
See especially Chapter 6: The English Civil War and the subjugation of Ireland.

J ENGBERG Royalist finances during the English Civil War. *Scandinavian Economic History Review* **XIV** No. 2 1966:73−96

(A EYRE) *A Dyurnall or Catalogue of all my Accions and expences from the 1st of January 1646*. Surtees Society **65** 1875 (pub. 1877).
Diary of a South Yorkshire yeoman, Adam Eyre.

C H FIRTH Sir Hugh Chomley's narrative of the Siege of Scarborough, 1644−5. *English Historical Review* **32** 1917:568−87

S R GARDNER *A History of the Great Civil War, 1642−1649*. (3 vols.) London:1886−91 (also reissued in 4 vols. 1894). Reprinted, Windrush:1987

J G GOUGH *The Superlative Prodigall: a Life of Thomas Bushell*. Bristol: 1932.

C P HILL *Who's Who in Stuart Britain*. Revised Ed. London:1988

C HOLMES *The Eastern Association in the English Civil War*. Cambridge: 1974

R HUTTON *The Royalist War Effort 1642−1646*. London:1982

S JEFFERSON (ed) *A Narrative of the Siege of Carlisle in 1644 and 1645 by Isaac Tullie*. Carlisle:1840

O MILLAR *The Age of Charles I: painting in England 1620−1649*. London (Tate Gallery):1972

R OLLARD *This War Without an Enemy*. London:1976
Well-illustrated general account.
D PARSONS (ed) *The Diary of Sir Henry Slingsby, of Scriven, Bart*.
London:1836
Includes an informative Civil War narrative of events in Yorkshire and
elsewhere, and extracts from household accounts.
M ROGERS *William Dobson 1611–46*. London (National Portrait Gal-
lery): 1983
A major exhibition of royalist portraits.
C V WEDGWOOD *The King's Peace, 1637–1641* London 1955; *The
King's War, 1641–1647*. London:1958

Numismatic and related works

D F ALLEN The 'Weymouth' and 'Salisbury' mints of Charles I. *British
Numismatic Journal* **23** 1938–40:97–118
G BERRY *Seventeenth Century England: Traders and their Tokens*. London:
1988
E M BESLY The York Mint of Charles I. *British Numismatic Journal* **54**
1984:210–41
E M BESLY *English Civil War Coin Hoards*. British Museum Occasional
Paper **51** London:1987
E M BESLY Rotary coining in Britain. *Metallurgy in Numismatics* **III**
forthcoming (Proceedings of a Symposium at the British Museum,
September 1988)
G C BOON *Cardiganshire Silver and the Aberystwyth Mint in Peace and
War*. Cardiff:1981 (with reprints of Bushell's mining pamphlets
and full bibliography)
C E CHALLIS *et al A New History of the Royal Mint*. Cambridge: forth-
coming
M COATE The royalist mints of Truro and Exeter 1642–6. *Numismatic
Chronicle* (5th Ser.) **8** 1928:213–48
D R COOPER *The Art and Craft of Coinmaking: a History of Minting
Technology*. London:1988
A DOWLE and P FINN *The Guide Book to the Coinage of Ireland, from 995
A.D. to the present day*. London:1969
H FARQUHAR Nicholas Briot and the Civil War. *Numismatic Chronicle*
(4th Ser.) **14** 1914:169–235
H FARQUHAR A lost coinage in the Channel Islands. *Numismatic Chro-
nicle* (5th Ser.) **8** 1928:199–212
J D GOULD The Royal Mint in the early seventeenth century. *Economic
History Review* (2nd Ser.) **5** 1952–3:240–8

E HAWKINS *Medallic Illustrations of the History of Great Britain and Ireland to the death of George II.* (edited by A.L. Franks and H.A. Grueber) **I** London:1885
Despite its title, has few pictures. A fully illustrated companion edition, but with edited text, was published in parts, 1904−11 and reprinted in one volume by Seaby in 1979.

H R JESSOP Flans for Newark Siege Coins. *Spink's Numismatic Circular* **March** 1976:90−1

M JONES *The Art of the Medal.* London:1979
Chapter 8 (pp. 65−74) deals with English medals before 1660.

M LESSEN The Cromwell Dunbar medals by Simon. *British Numismatic Journal* **51** 1981:112−33

R LYALL The Chester Mint and the coins attributed to that mint. *Spink's Numismatic Circular* **March** 1971:98−9

A J NATHANSON *Thomas Simon. His Life and Work 1618−1665.* London: 1975

J J NORTH *English Hammered Coinage, Vol. II: Edward I to Charles II, 1272−1662.* 2nd Ed. London:1975

J J NORTH and P J PRESTON-MORLEY *Sylloge of Coins of the British Isles 33: The John G. Brooker Collection, Coins of Charles I.* London: 1984
Includes essays on the Tower Mint (by J P C Kent) and Provincial and Civil War issues (by G C Boon) and a comprehensive numismatic bibliography to 1983.

C OMAN A note on the coining of the royal plate at Newark in the Year 1646. *Numismatic Chronicle* (5th Ser.) **14** 1934:74−80

(B A SEABY LTD) *Coins of England and the United Kingdom.* (25th Ed) London:1989

P SEABY and P F PURVEY *Coins of Scotland, Ireland & the Islands.* London: 1984

D SELLWOOD The trial of Nicholas Briot. *British Numismatic Journal* **56** 1986:108−23
English translation of the report of a trial of Briot's coining methods in Paris in 1617.

M B SHARP The Tower shillings of Charles I and their influence on the Aberystwyth issue. *British Numismatic Journal* **47** 1977:102−13

H SYMONDS Charles I: the trials of the pyx, the mint-marks and the mint accounts. *Numismatic Chronicle* (4th Ser.) **10** 1910:388−97

Index

Notes: references are to the page number; those in bold are to the illustration number, Roman numerals referring to colour plate numbers.